At the Heart of Generosity

John Jonez

"At the Heart of Generosity: What Jesus Actually Said About Money is a compelling and insightful guide to understanding Jesus' teachings on money and the existing strongholds that must be demolished to fulfill our purpose of living as faithful stewards. It is a must-read for anyone seeking to align their financial life with their spiritual values. It offers inspiration and actionable steps for living a free and generous life."

Leo Sabo, President, Christian Stewardship Network

"At the Heart of Generosity is best read with a reflective, devotional posture. John's clear, profound approach to stewardship will inspire readers in any financial circumstance to consider how their use of money honors God. Since biblical generosity is a pathway to greater intimacy with God, this book will encourage deeper devotion to our gracious Lord for all who give it their attention!"

Ryan Assunto, President, National Christian Foundation, Austin & Central Texas

"John brings the much-needed spiritual 'why' for the practical 'how' of managing God's money. Satan would love more than just about anything for God's children to live as though money had no spiritual impact. John reveals the truth of God's word: how we view and use money has as much of an impact on our spiritual growth as prayer, reading the Bible, attending church, and worship."

Donna Nicholson Stief, Director of Stewardship at LCBC Church and Board Member, Christian Stewardship Network.

"It's easy to forget that the Bible has so much to say about money and the place it holds in our hearts. John takes the time to present a balanced equation of both practical tools and Biblical truth, bringing a complete picture to the healthy role money can play in our lives."

Amy Neading, Adult Ministry Director, Hill Country Bible Church

"John Jonez offers Christians caught up in the ways of the world a clear path to repentance. A deeper discipleship can only be reached by addressing the worldly power of mammon in our lives. By wrestling with biblical stories and commands, Christians can move away from the anxiety of a "Lifestyle First" mentality toward a "Giving First" mentality that creates true joy."

Scott Kubie, CFA. President, Orchard Alliance

"At The Heart of Generosity is a wonderfully refreshing work on the significance and importance of giving and generosity. A detailed analysis of Scripture yields a practical tool that anyone can use in a small group or discipleship group setting to promote spiritual growth through Biblical stewardship. I highly recommend this book to all who are serious about living generous lives and helping others grow in the grace of giving."

Chuck Barber, Cohort Coach, Church Evangelism Institute

"I have read a lot of books about God and money, and this book takes a distinctly different approach. John gets at the heart of why we might fall prey to money's temptations. John's book is filled with Scripture and will fuel your love for God and generosity. I especially loved the sample prayers, sprinkled throughout the book, guiding us to actively engage with the scriptural truths."

Deb Gore, Executive Board Chair, National Christian Foundation, Austin, Texas

"At the Heart of Generosity explores the joys and spiritual significance of biblical generosity, balancing inspiration with caution rooted in Scripture. It's practical and insightful, encouraging readers to cultivate a generous heart where ultimate freedom and joy are found."

David Gonzales, Business Owner, Entrepreneur, and former EVP at Generous Giving

"John's thoughtfulness on generously is a heartfelt and insightful guide that explores the true essence of giving beyond material wealth. What makes this book stand out is John's ability to weave his personal journey into God's heart, making it relatable and deeply inspiring. His passion for generosity shines through, encouraging readers to adopt a mindset of abundance and selflessness. A must-read for anyone looking to lead a more generous and fulfilling life."

Trey Campbell, Senior Partner, Generous Giving

"Scripturally rooted and practically oriented, John has put within these pages a comprehensive and yet accessible treatment of generosity. I recently came across yet another set of statistics that further show our culture's idolatrous bent to be anything but generous. In contrast, John so helpfully lays out, generosity is not only reflective of the heart of our giving to God, but it's our path to share that very heart. Generosity is a key component to looking more like Jesus. In the paradox of how God has set up life, accumulation leads us away from what we truly want, while generosity leads us to it. Do we ever need such a call today!"

Eric Creekmore, Executive Director, Association of Hill Country Churches

"At the Heart of Generosity is a transformational road map, rooted in Scripture and teachings of Christ, which will take you on an expedient journey to becoming a grateful and generous giver. With impeccable insight, John lays out a straightforward path that, if followed, will have an immensely positive impact for God's Kingdom. As readers embark on this journey, they will discover the power of gratitude transforming their perception, strengthening their faith and developing a deeper relationship with God."

Theo Smith, Pastor of Stewardship (retired), Certified Financial Planner

"John Jonez has created an incredible experience with *At the Heart of Generosity*. In my almost 30 years of ministry, I have never seen anything like this. We have so many how to books about generosity but not much deals with the heart. John's God-given ability, mixed with his experience in finance, allows him to break things down in a way that people can understand in tangible and powerful ways. You will surely feel his heart and passion for issues around why God wants us to be generous."

Aaron Foor, Pastor & Church Advance for the Christian and Missionary Alliance

"At the Heart of Generosity is a reminder that we are made in God's image, which means we are to grow to be a generous giver just like Him. John leads the readers to become more aware of the spiritual undercurrents of the Enemy, who wants to steer us away from God and His Word. He then leads us through Scripture to understand what biblical generosity looks like and how generosity grows through a transformed heart like His."

Lee Ann Penick, Certified Public Accountant

At the Heart of Generosity: What Jesus Actually Said about Money
First Edition, 2024
Copyright © 2024 by John Jonez

All rights reserved. No part of this publication may be reproduced, stored in a retrieval system, or transmitted in any form by any means—electronic, mechanical, photocopy, recording, or otherwise—except for brief quotations in critical reviews or articles, without the prior permission of the publisher, except as provided by U.S. copyright law.

Scriptures marked AMP are taken from the AMPLIFIED BIBLE (AMP): Scripture taken from the AMPLIFIED® BIBLE, Copyright © 1954, 1958, 1962, 1964, 1965, 1987 by the Lockman Foundation (www.Lockman.org). Used by Permission.

Scriptures marked ESV are taken from THE HOLY BIBLE, ENGLISH STANDARD VERSION® Copyright© 2001 by Crossway, a publishing ministry of Good News Publishers. Used by permission. Scriptures marked KJV are taken from the KING JAMES VERSION (KJV): KING JAMES VERSION. Public Domain.

Scriptures marked NASB are taken from the NEW AMERICAN STANDARD (NAS): Scripture taken from the NEW AMERICAN STANDARD BIBLE®, copyright© 1960, 1962, 1963, 1968, 1971, 1972, 1973, 1975, 1977, 1995 by The Lockman Foundation. Used by permission.

Scriptures marked NIV are taken from the NEW INTERNATIONAL VERSION (NIV): Scripture taken from THE HOLY BIBLE, NEW INTERNATIONAL VERSION ®. Copyright© 1973, 1978, 1984, 2011 by Biblica, Inc.™. Used by permission of Zondervan.

Scriptures marked NKJV are taken from the NEW KING JAMES VERSION (NKJV): Scripture taken from the NEW KING JAMES VERSION®. Copyright© 1982 by Thomas Nelson, Inc. Used by permission. All rights reserved.

Scriptures marked NLT are taken from the HOLY BIBLE, NEW LIVING TRANSLATION (NLT): Scriptures taken from the HOLY BIBLE, NEW LIVING TRANSLATION, Copyright© 1996, 2004, 2007 by Tyndale House Foundation. Used by permission of Tyndale House Publishers, Inc., Carol Stream, Illinois 60188. All rights reserved. Used by permission.

Scriptures marked RSV are taken from the REVISED STANDARD VERSION (RSV): Scripture taken from the REVISED STANDARD VERSION, Grand Rapids: Zondervan, 1971.

Words of Christ are denoted in red.

To order additional books:
www.generousheart.com
www.amazon.com

Discounts available for bulk orders; please inquire.

To learn more, visit:
www.generousheart.com

ISBN: 978-1-952943-50-8

Editorial and Book Packaging: Inspira Literary Solutions, Gig Harbor, WA
Book Design: Brianna Showalter

Printed in the USA

CONTENTS

FOREWORD [7]
INTRODUCTION [9]

SECTION ONE [10]
Our Practical and Divinely Powerful Tools

SECTION TWO [21]
Two Masters, One Lord
Stronghold – "Mammon and His Influence"

SECTION THREE [30]
God Owns Everything; We Are His Managers
Stronghold – "Excessive Focus on Money"

SECTION FOUR [46]
Giving Is an Act of Worship

SECTION FIVE [56]
Generosity: The Evidence of a Grateful Heart
Stronghold – "Inferior Motivations about Giving"

SECTION SIX [68]
What Does a Good Steward Look Like?

SECTION SEVEN [78]
Getting Practical: Where Do I Begin??
Stronghold – "Passivity"

GROUP DISCUSSION QUESTIONS [86]
APPENDIX [89]
Personal Money Management Assessment [90]
Spending Plan Worksheet [92]
Spending Plan Category Descriptions [94]
Spending Decision Tool [95]
Book Review – *The Golden Ghetto*, by Jessie O'Neill [96]
Giving Causes to Consider [97]

ABOUT THE AUTHOR [99]
ACKNOWLEDGMENTS [100]
ENDNOTES [101]

FOREWORD

By Mike Riches, D.Min.

It is with great pleasure that I write this foreword for *At the Heart of Generosity*. The Gospels record Jesus speaking more about finances than any other topic. It has been reported that they recount Jesus talking about finances seven times more often than the topics of heaven and hell together.

John's approach to personal finance in this manual is unique. He delves into the spiritual realities at the heart of money and financial management, a perspective rarely explored in financial training. His profound, biblically solid, and practical handling of this critical subject is sure to captivate and challenge readers.

John has extensive financial experience, having served as a Financial Executive for multiple successful organizations. His deep understanding of the practical and spiritual aspects of finance make him more than qualified to write this manual.

In At *the Heart of Generosity*, John doesn't just discuss finances; he offers a path to personal and financial transformation. His insights, rooted in the biblical perspective on money, are practical and profoundly transformative. They challenge readers to examine their hearts, their perspective about money, and their financial habits in light of God's Word, offering hope for a fresh start.

John's writing style is engaging, and his message is clear and compelling. As you engage with his teachings, you will find yourself inspired and equipped to approach your finances in a fresh way. Whether you are struggling with debt, seeking to increase your giving, or simply desiring to align your financial practices with your faith, *At the Heart of Generosity* will be invaluable.

I do not doubt that this book will bless all who read it, and I commend John for his dedication to sharing the truth about money from a bold, spiritual, and biblical framework. May you be encouraged as you embark on the journey into *At the Heart of Generosity*.

Mike Riches, D.Min.
Senior Pastor; Founder and Director of The Sycamore Commission; Author of *Living Set Free in Christ*

INTRODUCTION

If you look in the mirror, you probably see a person who looks fairly normal. But if the person looking back at you is a fully devoted follower of Jesus, he or she will have a difficult journey while on Earth. This world is full of darkness and cultural norms directly opposing Jesus' teaching on how we are to live.

But for His followers, this life culminates in a glorious eternity where we will experience unimaginable peace and joy with Him. For simplicity, we consider these worldly norms to be "distractions" along this journey. The most common distraction of all may very well be money, and all the issues surrounding it. It is likely the single most seductive and corrupting substance in our society.

At the Heart of Generosity is an exploration into God's original design for managing the financial resources He has entrusted to every follower of Christ. It dives into the spiritual and scriptural issues surrounding money, focusing on how, from the origins of the human race, God intended for His followers to view and manage it. A person's attitude about money, and behaviors with money, likely indicates their level of spiritual maturity in this area of their life. We present the spiritual tools found in Scripture for believers to use in finding freedom from the negative influences of money.

Scripture has over 2000 individual verses regarding the issues of money, wealth, possessions, and giving, so we should view it is a highly important topic to God. These verses provide both wisdom and warnings we can learn from and live by. Once that wisdom is embedded into our thinking and reflected in the actions of our daily lives, it leads to a journey of freedom, peace, and joy surpassing human understanding, and a deeply intimate relationship with God through Christ.

Psalm 119:130 (NIV)
The unfolding of your words gives light; it gives understanding to the simple.

This book focuses on what God wants for you—the true blessing of a God-given capacity to experience His joy and extend His goodness in this life. Regardless of whether God's blessings include external components, they are intended to bring about *internal* change so our lives transform into an ever-increasing reflection of the character of Jesus. It is written to stimulate the reader's self-discovery of the relationship between gratitude, generosity, and their own walk with Jesus. Gratitude is the source of all generosity, and generosity has the power to change the human heart.

Now, let's wrestle with the teachings of Jesus, look deeply *At the Heart of Generosity*, and discover what it means to "share in the joy of the Master" (Matthew 25:23).

SECTION ONE
Our Practical and Divinely Powerful Tools*

Managing money well requires many practical actions. Creating a budget and comparing it to our actual expenses, paying bills on time, spending less than our income, saving for the future, and investing wisely are just a few of these. But the bigger issues we will explore are the less-well-known *spiritual* issues about money. That is the primary focus of this study.

"Freedom" is at the heart of the life and message of Jesus Christ. Jesus said, *"If you hold to my teaching, you are really my disciples. Then you will know the truth and the truth will set you free"* (John 8:31b–32, NIV). The Apostle Paul reiterated, *"It is for freedom Christ has set us free"* (Galatians 5:1, NIV). Regarding money, it is the lack of understanding of the spiritual influences surrounding money, and the tools available to deal with those issues, that often robs us of the very freedom Jesus wants for us.

GOD'S ORIGINAL DESIGN

God's original design is that we would live eternally with Him in perfect unity and fellowship. We were created to be fulfilled, complete, joy-filled, and at peace, and in that to glorify God. He created mankind to dwell with Him.

*The content from this section is excerpted from the *Living Set Free in Christ Course Manual*, by Mike Riches, published by SycPub Global. Used by permission. www.sycpubglobal.com

GOD CREATED US TO BE IN AN INTIMATE, LOVING RELATIONSHIP WITH HIM.

Isaiah 54:10 (NIV)
Though the mountains be shaken and the hills be removed, yet my unfailing love for you will not be shaken nor my covenant of peace be removed," says the Lord.

GOD CREATED US FOR A PURPOSE.

Genesis 2:15 (NIV)
The LORD God took the man and put him in the Garden of Eden to work it and take care of it.

GOD CREATED US TO LIVE FREE

Genesis 2:25 (NIV)
Adam and his wife were naked, and they felt no shame.

Shortly thereafter, it all went wrong (Genesis 3:1–13). Adam and Eve disobeyed God and ate the fruit of the only forbidden tree in the Garden of Eden. This disobedience caused Adam to give up the right to live in God's original design, and it subsequently impacted every person in every generation to succeed him. Consequently, each of us has inherited a sin nature, compromising every aspect of God's purposes and plans for us, resulting in spiritual death and our lives being lived outside of His original design.

Romans 5:12 (NLT)
When Adam sinned, sin entered the world. Adam's sin brought death, so death spread to everyone, for everyone sinned.

HOW DO WE BECOME FREE AGAIN?

How do we walk out of the fallen state humanity finds itself in as a result of Adam's sin, and into the freedom God designed and desires for us? There is only one answer, and it could not be clearer—it begins with the person of Jesus Christ. The restoration of God's original design and to provide each of us a path back to be reconciled with the Father, is the reason Jesus came to Earth.

John 14:6 (NIV)
Jesus answered, "I am the way and the truth and the life. No one comes to the Father except through me."

Luke 19:10 (NASB)
For the Son of Man has come to seek and to save that which was lost.

> We were created to be fulfilled, complete, joy-filled, and at peace. God created mankind to dwell with Him.

> *"Human-Divine Cooperative"* — a work that only God can do is initiated when a person exercises his or her God-given responsibility.

John 3:16 (NIV)
For God so loved the world that he gave his one and only Son, that whoever believes in Him shall not perish but have eternal life.

THE HUMAN-DIVINE COOPERATIVE

The great gift of freedom is God's plan and His work. It is dependent on Him, and is only accomplished by Him. We do not have the capability to become righteous, as only God is righteous, yet we do have an important part to play. In order to receive this gift of freedom, we must choose to place our faith and trust in Jesus, and receive Him as our Lord and Savior.

John 1:12–13 (NIV)
Yet to all who did receive Him, to those who believed in His name, he gave the right to become children of God – children born not of natural descent, nor of human decision or a husband's will, but born of God.

We call this the "Human-Divine Cooperative"—that is, a work that only God can do is initiated when a person exercises his or her God-given responsibility. Said differently, "We must do what only we can do (choose and receive Jesus), so God will do what only God can do."

UNDERSTANDING "SPIRITUAL TRANSACTIONS"

In day-to-day life, when a business deal is agreed upon, a contract is signed and then sealed by a notary of the public. This creates a transaction whereby ownership is transferred. Similarly, on a spiritual level, when a follower of Jesus makes a determination of his or her will, based on truth, and then makes a faith-filled declaration with his or her words, it is sealed by the Authority (God) of the universe. A spiritual transaction is realized—it is done! This transaction takes place in the spiritual realm that has an impact here on Earth in the natural or physical realm.

The spiritual transaction fulfills a promise from God.

Matthew 16:19 (NIV)
I will give you the keys of the kingdom of heaven; whatever you bind on earth will be bound in heaven, and whatever you loose on earth will be loosed in heaven.

What we do here on Earth matters in Heaven.

Psalm 115:16 (NIV)
The highest heavens belong to the Lord, but the earth he has given to mankind.

Components of a spiritual transaction:
- Agree with the terms of God's truth.
- Submit to the terms of God's truth.
- Make a faith-filled declaration with your words.
- Understand it is backed by God's sovereign authority.
- Know that a spiritual transaction has taken place with God's power released in every real way.

OUR FIRST SPIRITUAL TRANSACTION

The very first spiritual transaction for a follower of Jesus is when a person receives Him as their Lord and Savior. It has all the components shown above present—it is based on truth we submit to, words are spoken, a prayer is made with conviction from the heart, and a transaction takes place that is sealed by the power and authority of God.

Romans 10:9 (NIV)
If you declare with your mouth, "Jesus is Lord," and believe in your heart that God raised him from the dead, you will be saved.

Examples of subsequent spiritual transactions:
- The exchange of vows and declaration of "husband and wife" in marriage
- Repentance of our sins
- Forgiveness of others
- Submission to Him as He calls us

ONE WORLD, TWO REALMS

The Bible teaches us that the world we live in has two realms. The first one is visible, physical, material, and natural, and we can perceive and interact with it by using our five senses. The other realm is spiritual and invisible often referred to as the "heavenlies" realm, where our five "natural" senses are useless. This second realm includes all that is spiritual, invisible, and not seen in the natural realm (e.g., God, Holy Spirit, angelic beings, demonic beings). The Apostle Paul wrote of this realm often, particularly in Ephesians, where he mentions it five times (Ephesians 1:3, 1:26, 2:6, 3:10, 6:12).

Being invisible to the naked eye does not make the "heavenlies" realm any less "real." These two realms are both real yet they are distinct, and operate concurrently in our lives. As believers, we live in both realms simultaneously. While we can see the battles and wars happening in our world, as followers of Jesus, we must also be fully aware of the reality of the spiritual realm where the spiritual battles take place, and their impact on us.

Ephesians 6:12 (NIV)
> *For our struggle is not against flesh and blood, but against the rulers, against the authorities, against the powers of this dark world and against the spiritual forces of evil in the heavenly realms.*

John 10:10 (NIV)
> *The thief comes only to steal and kill and destroy; I have come that they may have life, and have it to the full.*

1 John 3:8 (NIV)
> *The one who does what is sinful is of the devil, because the devil has been sinning from the beginning. The reason the Son of God appeared was to destroy the devil's work.*

> We live in one world that has two realms. As followers of Jesus, we live in both of them simultaneously.

THE BELIEVER'S AUTHORITY IN CHRIST

Living in God's supernatural authority is an amazing right and privilege of every Christian. Jesus promised it. Throughout His life, He demonstrated both power and authority. He resisted every temptation of Satan. He overpowered Satan's kingdom at every front, from healing people to delivering them from demonic assault. Where Jesus showed up, Satan fled!

JESUS HAS ULTIMATE AUTHORITY

Ephesians 1:19–22 (NLT)
I also pray that you will understand the incredible greatness of God's power for us who believe him. This is the same mighty power that raised Christ from the dead and seated him in the place of honor at God's right hand in the heavenly realms. Now he is far above any ruler or authority or power or leader or anything else—not only in this world but also in the world to come. God has put all things under the authority of Christ and has made him head over all things for the benefit of the church.

JESUS MINISTERED UNDER GOD'S AUTHORITY

John 5:30 (NLT)
I can do nothing on my own. I judge as God tells me. Therefore, my judgment is just, because I carry out the will of the one who sent me, not my own will.

BELIEVERS RECEIVE THIS POWER AND AUTHORITY AT SALVATION

Colossians 2:9–10 (NIV)
For in Christ all the fullness of the Deity lives in bodily form, and in Christ you have been brought to fullness. He is the head over every power and authority.

THROUGH THE LOVE OF CHRIST, WE ARE MADE COMPLETE IN HIS FULLNESS

Ephesians 3:19 (NLT)
May you experience the love of Christ, though it is too great to understand fully. Then you will be made complete with all the fullness of life and power that comes from God.

Jesus rules over the entire heavenlies realm, seated in the place of ultimate authority—at the right hand of His Father. At the time of our salvation, Jesus swept us up and seated

> *The authority given to Jesus by His Father has been given to us! Jesus fully intended for All his followers to share in His power and authority.*

us with Him in the heavenlies. This is a present reality, not one that will be realized only in the future. We NOW possess every spiritual blessing in the heavenlies, through Christ. This means the authority given to Jesus by His Father has also been given to us!

Ephesians 2:4–6 (NIV)
But because of his great love for us, God, who is rich in mercy, made us alive with Christ even when we were dead in transgressions—it is by grace you have been saved and God raised us up with Christ and seated us with him in the heavenly realms in Christ Jesus.

WE ARE TO CARRY OUT CHRIST'S WORK UNDER THE AUTHORITY OF JESUS

Matthew 28:18–19 (NLT)
Jesus came and told his disciples, "I have been given all authority in heaven and on earth. Therefore, go and make disciples of all the nations, baptizing them in the name of the Father and the Son and the Holy Spirit."

WE ARE TO PROACTIVELY EXERCISE OUR AUTHORITY IN CHRIST

James 4:7 (NIV)
Submit yourselves, then, to God. Resist the devil, and he will flee from you.

UNDERSTANDING SPIRITUAL STRONGHOLDS AND HOW THEY ARE BUILT

Stronghold (Definition) – "Thoughts, beliefs, philosophies, attitudes, and values that oppose God's truth. This truth can be regarding God, how God regards humans (especially "you"), about Jesus Christ (what He has done for you and how He lives for you), who and what you are, what you possess, how life is to be lived, and/or regarding what truly brings fullness and freedom in life and what results in bondage, ruin, and destruction."

2 Corinthians 10:3–5 (NIV)
For though we live in the world, we do not wage war as the world does. The weapons we fight with are not the weapons of the world. On the contrary, they have divine power to demolish strongholds. We

demolish arguments and every pretension that sets itself up against the knowledge of God, and we take captive every thought to make it obedient to Christ.

Scripture tells us in this passage we can be taken captive by wrong thinking—and we are held there by "strongholds."

God's truth is Absolute. Every degree to which we are out of alignment with or oppose God's truth, on every issue in life, gives Satan an opportunity to establish his influence in our lives. Allowing the enemy to have this "opportunity," "place," "foothold," or "territory" (the Greek word originally used in this passage is *topos*), gives him jurisdiction—or the legal right—to operate in our life in ways that completely oppose God's truth.

It is our own sin, or our sinful responses to the actions of other people, that relinquishes this jurisdiction to Satan, and a stronghold is established. Strongholds originate in our thoughts that are opposed to God's truth, then manifest themselves in our actions, often before we are aware of it, and thereby we are taken captive and held in bondage to them.

Ephesians 4:26–27 (NIV)
"In your anger do not sin": Do not let the sun go down while you are still angry, and do not give the devil a foothold.

We cannot be naïve about this reality. Scripture warns us that the intentions of Satan are not friendly; they are aggressive and evil.

1 Peter 5:8 (NIV)
Be alert and of sober mind. Your enemy the devil prowls around like a roaring lion looking for someone to devour.

Once established, strongholds stop us from living out God's original design for our lives, and prevent us from receiving His mercy and grace. They obstruct and distract us from living lives in God's love and power to carry out His Kingdom mission on Earth.

Thankfully, in His infinite care and wisdom, God has given us clear direction and divinely powerful weapons, enabling us to live free in His truth and love.

> "Strongholds" are thoughts, beliefs, philosophies, attitudes, and values opposing God's truth.

© John Jonez 2024. All Rights Reserved.

DISMANTLING STRONGHOLDS

As we know, Satan is still as crafty as he was in the Garden of Eden, seeking to establish an evil influence in our lives, starting where ever we are most vulnerable. To find real freedom from any stronghold, the effort cannot be a passive one, it must be intentional and rigorous. Remember, we are not battling flesh and blood, but the forces of darkness in the spiritual realm. (Ephesians 6:12).

God, in His grace and mercy towards us, has provided spiritual weapons for us to use. He wants us free to be fully devoted to Him, and to live in the freedom of His love.

2 Corinthians 10:3–5 (NASB)
For though we walk in the flesh, we do not wage battle according to the flesh, for the weapons of our warfare are not of the flesh, but divinely powerful for the destruction of fortresses. We are destroying arguments and all arrogance raised against the knowledge of God, and we are taking every thought captive to the obedience of Christ.

The foundational posture for demolishing strongholds is our repentance. Repentance is not simply a sense of sorrow and an apology, but rather a privileged gift from God which unlocks the door to His forgiveness, freedom, and knowledge of the truth.

Acts 11:18b (NASB)
Well then, God has also granted to the Gentiles the repentance that leads to life.

Romans 2:4 (NASB)
Or do you think lightly of the riches of His kindness and restraint and patience, not knowing that the kindness of God leads you to repentance?

True repentance literally means "a change of mind," and a turn from one thing toward something different. It requires a change of values, belief system, and lifestyle, in order to turn away from sin. Scripture is clear that it is dangerous not to replace confessed sin with righteous behavior, or the enemy will return to reoccupy the vacuum left by confession unaccompanied by genuine repentance.

Consider this vivid example:

Matthew 12:43–45 (NLT)
When an evil spirit leaves a person, it goes into the desert, seeking rest but finding none. Then it says, "'I will return to

> *We live in a world of flesh and blood, but our battle is fundamentally spiritual and must be fought with spiritual weapons.*

the person I came from.'" So it returns and finds its former home empty, swept, and in order. Then the spirit finds seven other spirits more evil than itself, and they all enter the person and live there. And so that person is worse off than before. That will be the experience of this evil generation.

This state of genuine repentance is all about the heart (see James chapter 4), and requires the following posture:
1. A heart of humility (James 4:6)
2. A heart of submission (James 4:7–9)
3. A heart of confession and repentance (James 4:8b–9)
4. A heart of aggressive resistance (James 4:7)
5. The promise: the devil will flee from you (James 4:7b)

James 4:7 (NIV)
Submit yourselves, then, to God. Resist the devil, and he will flee from you.

Jesus demonstrated many times what it looks like to receive and live in God's authority. He showed He not only had the power of God in His life, but also the permission to use it and share it—first with his 12 disciples, and then to 72 others.

Luke 9:1 (NASB)
Now He called the twelve together and gave them power and authority over all the demons, and the power to heal diseases.

Luke 10:17–19 (NLT)
When the seventy-two disciples returned, they joyfully reported to him, "Lord, even the demons obey us when we use your name!" "Yes," he told them, *"I saw Satan fall from heaven like lightning! Look, I have given you authority over all the power of the enemy, and you can walk among snakes and scorpions and crush them. Nothing will injure you."*

© John Jonez 2024. All Rights Reserved.

THE 4RS

The "4Rs" is a model of prayer to help us remember God's truths, outlined in this section, in order to demolish strongholds and move into God's freedom through spiritual transactions in a human-divine cooperative, as we discussed earlier. These steps in this model include:

1. REPENT and receive the Lord's forgiveness.

Acts 3:19 (NIV)
Repent, then, and turn to God, so that your sins may be wiped out, that times of refreshing may come from the Lord,

2. REBUKE demonic influences and renounce the lies contradicting God's truth.

Matthew 4:10 (NIV)
Jesus said to him, "Away from me, Satan! For it is written: 'Worship the Lord your God, and serve him only.'"

3. REPLACE Satan's lies and renew your commitment to walk in the truth.

Ephesians 4:22—24 (NIV)
You were taught, with regard to your former way of life, to put off your old self, which is being corrupted by its deceitful desires; to be made new in the attitude of your minds; and to put on the new self, created to be like God in true righteousness and holiness.

4. RECEIVE the infilling work of God's Spirit, and rejoice in it.

Ephesians 5:18 (NLT)
Don't be drunk with wine, because that will ruin your life. Instead, be filled with the Holy Spirit.

Titus 3:4–6 (NIV)
But when the kindness and love of God our Savior appeared, he saved us, not because of righteous things we had done, but because of his mercy. He saved us through the washing of rebirth and renewal by the Holy Spirit, whom he poured out on us generously through Jesus Christ our Savior.

Throughout the rest of this study, we will practice using these tools and executing spiritual transactions, in order to demolish the strongholds related to money in our lives.

SECTION TWO
Two Masters, One Lord

A BRIEF HISTORY OF MONEY

In today's world, we use money almost every day, although various forms of electronic payment have largely replaced the use of paper currency and coins. The use of credit has become so common for everyday expenditures that many people focus on the affordability of "monthly payments" rather than the actual price of an item they want to purchase.

Back in ancient history, the use of a government-issued currency to conduct commerce did not exist. Most common was a practice of bartering with one another to buy and sell things. Trading leather and furs for spices and food was normal, and trading your labor for hard goods was common. In today's world, try to imagine bartering as the only way to buy and sell. Consider one person owning a car dealership, and another who owns an ice cream shop. How could a person acquire a Toyota by trading for ice cream cones? The relative values are so different it would be virtually impossible—a lifetime of ice cream cones?

As bartering became more problematic, gold and silver emerged as the most common form of "currency" to transact purchases and sales, because of their universally accepted value. Somewhere between

1100BC and 650BC, government-issued "coins" were developed and became widely accepted as a "medium of exchange." Today the US dollar has zero *intrinsic* value; it is just a piece of paper, created on a fancy printer, that is extremely difficult to duplicate. It is accepted for its face value because it is backed by "the full faith and credit of the United States government."

BENEFICIAL USES OF MONEY

Having money definitely has advantages, especially when compared to not having any money. The most specific and fundamental problem money can solve is the problem of survival. Of course, this assumes a person has access to basic goods and services, such as food, water, shelter, clothing, and medical care. If a person is struggling literally for "life-or-death" survival, they have one and only one problem to solve, and no other problem is relevant. For billions of people in the world, basic survival is at risk.

Other beneficial uses of money include the purchase of our needs and wants, use as a tool to accumulate and store wealth, and the ability to offer help to others through generous giving.

THE DOWNSIDE OF MONEY

We have all heard the expression "money talks," which means wealth can have a great influence on people. This can be good, but this can also mean money can change our behavior in a negative way. It has the power to control us, possibly making us greedy, selfish, or prideful. It can definitely compete for our affection or become an idol. Money can make us believe that it alone will buy happiness. It won't.

THE ALMIGHTY DOLLAR

The term "the almighty dollar" is most commonly attributed to the American author Washington Irving in his short story called "The Creole Village," first published in 1837.[1] Irving's quote became famous: "The Almighty Dollar, that great object of universal devotion throughout our land."

The term has become common today, in a figurative way, to signify an obsession with money, or more broadly, with material wealth. Similar to the term "money talks," "the almighty dollar" is meant to project influence, control, or significance. The term "almighty," in conjunction with any other word, implies power or deity.

THE WORDS OF JESUS

In Matthew 5, 6, and 7, Jesus delivers the most famous and compelling sermon ever given in the history of the world, which we know as "The Sermon on the Mount": three full chapters of His words, outlining the standards of behavior for His followers. His expectations substantially raised the bar well above the law the Jewish people had come to know. It also contains several parables, wisdom, and even how we are to pray, giving us The Lord's Prayer.

> "I made my first investment at age 11. I was wasting my life up until then."
>
> — Warren Buffett, the greatest investor to ever live.

The Sermon on the Mount includes these words:

Matthew 6:24 (NIV)
No one can serve two masters. Either you will hate the one and love the other, or you will be devoted to the one and despise the other. You cannot serve both God and money."

These are the words of Jesus, which we will wrestle with throughout this book. The last sentence of this verse is worded differently in other translations of the Bible:

NASB: *"You cannot serve both God and wealth."*
"Wealth" is a term that is broader than "money."

NLT: *"You cannot serve God and be enslaved to money."*
"Enslaved to money" implies an influencing behavior.

KJV, NKJV, and RSV: *"You cannot serve God and Mammon."*

© John Jonez 2024. All Rights Reserved.

One of the earliest English Bibles—*The Great Bible*—published in 1539, also uses the word "**Mammon**" in this verse.[2] Consider a few critically important aspects contained in this passage:

1. Because this verse is included in Jesus' most famous sermon, the content of it must be *highly important* for His followers to understand.

2. <u>"Two Masters"</u> – This is the only place in all of Scripture where Jesus compares two masters, side-by-side, and one of those masters is God Himself! He makes it clear we cannot serve them both, and our affection for one master would be the exact the opposite for the other—*loving* one and *hating* the other, or *devoted* to one and *despising* the other. This comparison is not subtle! Because we cannot simultaneously serve both masters, we must make a choice. That choice has an eternal impact.

3. <u>"Serving a Master"</u> – This refers to only one Master, not two. The idea of serving any master involves submission, obedience, and putting the Master's wishes ahead of our own. When considering God as our Master, it makes sense; it is what He asks us to do, because He created us with an original design, and He wants the best for us—always.

Now consider "money," a simple piece of paper covered with green ink, an inanimate object—how could it be a master? After all, it is just a physical thing, right? Money doesn't have a mind of its own, so how could it be influential as a "master" to be served? Why would Jesus compare it to God as an alternate master? He could have compared

"You cannot serve both God and Mammon"
- Jesus, in Matthew 6:24

anything else to God as a master. Maybe money really is irresistible.

WHAT IS "MAMMON"? OR WHO IS "MAMMON"?

When Jesus delivered this sermon, He spoke in His native language of Aramaic. He used the word *Mammon*, and His listeners understood this word. When the word *Mammon* was translated from Aramaic to Greek, the word used in Greek was *Mammon*, and when it was first translated from Greek to English, the word was still "Mammon."

Why was this word not translated into the different languages? It is because the word "Mammon" is a name—the name of an evil spirit, a demonic spirit, or a false god. Mammon is a "being," a spirit with the power to influence people. The following is a deeper look into what characterizes "Mammon":

- Synonyms: money, wealth, riches, possessions, treasure, greed
- Treasure or riches that are opposed to God
- The idol of materialism
- Wealth regarded as an evil influence
- The demon of wealth
- A false object of worship and devotion
- That in which one puts trust (money, riches)
- An evil spirit

Mammon, the demon of wealth, is depicted in this painting as a monstrous figure overseeing his fan club, who are too caught up in their riches to notice they're in the demon's den.

The Worship of Mammon, Evelyn De Morgan, c. 1909

Mammon: (Definition) – "The force and power around money that can change our thinking and behavior"[3]

God *does* care what we do with our money, but He cares far more about what our money does to us, due to the influence of Mammon.

What do we do about Mammon's evil influence in our life?

There is hope!

Ephesians 6:12 (NIV)
For our struggle is not against flesh and blood, but against the rulers, against the authorities, against the powers of this dark world and against the spiritual forces of evil in the heavenly realms.

© John Jonez 2024. All Rights Reserved.

Two Masters Comparison

Almighty Father (God)		Almighty Dollar (Mammon)
A Jealous Master who wants our Full Affection and Devotion	< The Same >	A Jealous Master who wants our Full Affection and Devotion
The Source of all TRUTH - truth that will set us free. (John 8:32)	< Opposite >	Subservient to Satan, The Father of LIES (John 8:44)
The Perfect Father who Created us, loves us, and sent his Son who came so that "we may have life, and have it abundantly" (John 10:10)	< Opposite >	A THIEF who comes only to Kill, Steal, and Destroy. (John 10:10)
Creator who brings LIGHT and LIFE	< Opposite >	Deceiver who brings DARKNESS and DEATH
Promises & Delivers Peace and Joy	< Opposite >	Promises Power, Status, Fulfillment, Happiness. Delivers Anxiety & Emptiness
Focus is what He wants FOR us	< Opposite >	Focus is what he wants FROM us
Followers may become Humble and Generous	< Opposite >	Followers may become Prideful and Selfish
Worthy of our Trust and Devotion	< Opposite >	Worthy of our Distrust and Rejection
We must CHOOSE to Follow this Master	< Opposite >	We may Follow this Master our entire lifetime without knowing it

Which Master is more powerful? The one you follow.

DISCOVERING AND DEMOLISHING STRONGHOLDS

STRONGHOLD: MAMMON

Mammon's desires are purely evil. His singular mission is to *entice* us away from following God, *deceive* us about God's truths—replacing them with his lies—and *prevent* us from living out those truths in our daily life. Mammon is an evil spirit, who is "alive and well" today, seeking to destroy God's people.

You may have never heard of Mammon, and if you have heard of him, you may never have considered whether this evil spirit has any influence in your life. Here are some diagnostic statements to help you assess:

DIAGNOSTIC STATEMENTS

- ❏ I have been stressed about money.
- ❏ I think, or have thought, my problems would go away with "just a little more money."
- ❏ I do or have felt secure because I earn a high income.
- ❏ I feel some reluctance when I think about giving money away.
- ❏ I do not faithfully give away the "first and best" of what I earn.
- ❏ I do not pray about things God wants me to give to.
- ❏ My giving is somewhat inconsistent.
- ❏ I struggle to save money for anything.
- ❏ I often buy things I want and quickly realize I don't really want them after all.
- ❏ Buying things makes me feel better.
- ❏ Credit card debt is a regular part of my life.
- ❏ My scarcity of money is on my mind constantly.
- ❏ My abundance of money is on my mind constantly.
- ❏ I live with a nagging anxiety about money.

These statements seem like money issues, but they are actually the tests of our faith in God as our ultimate provider. These thoughts and behaviors are caused by the influence of Mammon; therefore, Mammon may have created a "stronghold" in your life.

SPIRITUAL TRANSACTION USING THE 4RS PRAYER MODEL

1. <u>REPENT</u> – Turn away from Mammon's influence, and toward God.

   Sample Prayer – Father, we turn our eyes and hearts to You right now. We surrender to You all of our finances and everything You have given us. In humility, we submit our hearts to You. We repent for the times in our life where we chose Money or possessions to become a distraction or an idol, and it prevented us from putting You first, and experiencing the goodness You desire for us. We acknowledge this as sin, and ask for Your forgiveness for it.

2. <u>REBUKE</u> – Rebuke Mammon and every other evil spirit influencing this area of your life.

   Sample Prayer – Jesus, You have been given all authority on Heaven and Earth, and You have passed that authority onto us. In Your powerful name, we rebuke the evil spirit of Mammon right now and renounce all of his lies. We break off Mammon's influence in our lives and in the lives of our families, now and forever.

3. <u>REPLACE</u> – Replace every lie of Mammon and every false thought with God's truth.

   Sample Prayer – We replace Mammon's evil mission in our life with Your truth: You are the one and only Master we will follow. We are Your handiwork, created in Christ Jesus to do good works You have prepared for us, and we accept every part of those works.

4. <u>RECEIVE</u> – Receive the Lord's promise of forgiveness, His truth, and a fresh infilling of the Holy Spirit.

Sample Prayer – We ask to receive Your Holy Spirit, to fill us in every place previously occupied by the lies and evil thoughts of Mammon. We allow Your Holy Spirit to guide us to be faithful and trustworthy managers with all that You have entrusted to us, and to live generously at every opportunity. In Jesus' name, Amen.

It may not be obvious to you right now, but if you identified areas in your life influenced by Mammon, prayed this prayer with conviction from your heart, in humility meant every word, and have truly committed to follow God as your only Master, then you just put to work the tools covered in Section I of this study. You have demolished the stronghold of Mammon in your life, by executing a spiritual transaction that is bound in Heaven.

It is important to note that each of us may have to repeat this process on an ongoing basis. Keep in mind, "freedom" does not mean we will never have to deal with any of these issues again. Freedom means they will no longer control you. We may frequently sense the influence of Mammon in our lives, and will have to repent of that sin again. Over time, it will become increasingly easy to recognize Mammon's influence taking hold in our thoughts, and execute a new spiritual transaction to make those thoughts "obedient to Christ." This will keep them from making their way into our outward actions.

PRACTICAL APPLICATION – WALKING IN THE OPPOSITE DIRECTION

- ❑ I will recommit each day to God in prayer that He is my one-and-only Master.

- ❑ I will recommit each day to God in prayer that He owns everything, as I learn to become His faithful and trustworthy manager.

- ❑ I will internalize in my heart, and execute actions by my will, that demonstrate my security is in Him alone.

- ❑ I will continually pray for His Holy Spirit to guide me in managing the finances entrusted to me.

- ❑ I will commit to get professional help as needed to better manage the finances He has entrusted to me.

- ❑ Each day I will verbalize my gratitude for His provision, whatever that may be.

SECTION THREE
God Owns Everything; We Are His Managers

There is a tremendous difference between being an "owner" and being a "manager." Ownership involves the legal right to possess and control something, and the sole right to legally use it as we choose. The owner has full authority over something, and can choose to keep it, sell it, or give it away. Ownership can involve "real property" such as real estate, "personal property" like a car or set of golf clubs, or ownership in a company, partnership, or other intangible rights.

In contrast, a "manager" is a role each of us may fulfill in a variety of situations. For example, if you borrow your friend's car, you have some responsibility to "manage" or take care of it. If you lead a project at a company you work for, you have a responsibility to manage the project to a desired outcome on behalf of the company.

The highest level of expectation of any manager is called a "fiduciary"—that is, someone who is *legally required* to act in the best interest of the owner. In such a case, the person must be named in the role of a fiduciary, and must accept or decline the responsibilities accompanying that role. For example, when money is deposited at a bank, by law the bank must act as a fiduciary on behalf of the depositor. In all of these cases of being a manager or fiduciary, the person or institution is not an owner, but rather a manager.

SCRIPTURE IS CLEAR: GOD IS THE OWNER OF EVERYTHING

For most people, believing that God *created* everything is intuitive and fairly easy to accept. But, the idea that "God *owns* everything" may be a new concept. However, Scripture leaves no doubt about God's sovereign ownership over all Creation.

WE SEE THIS IN THE BEGINNING OF SCRIPTURE

Genesis 1:1 (NIV)
In the beginning God created the heavens and the earth.

THE PSALMS CONFIRM GOD'S SOVEREIGN OWNERSHIP

Psalm 24:1 (NIV)
The earth is the Lord's, and everything in it, the world and all who live in it.

Psalm 50:10–12 (NIV)
Every animal of the forest is mine, and the cattle on a thousand hills. I know every bird in the mountains, and the insects in the field are mine. The world is mine and all that is in it.

PAUL ACKNOWLEDGES GOD AS CREATOR OF ALL THINGS

Ephesians 3:9 (NLT)
I was chosen to explain to everyone this mysterious plan that God, the Creator of all things, had kept secret from the beginning.

JOB CONFIRMS GOD'S OWNERSHIP AND LORDSHIP

Job 1:21 (NIV)
Naked I came from my mother's womb, and naked I will depart. The Lord gave and the Lord has taken away; may the name of the Lord be praised.

PAUL CONFIRMS THE SUPREMACY OF JESUS

Colossians 1:15–17 (NLT)
Christ is the visible image of the invisible God. He existed before anything was created and is supreme over all creation, for through him God created everything in the heavenly realms and on earth. He made the things we can see and the things we can't see—such as thrones, kingdoms, rulers, and authorities in the unseen world.

Scripture is clear: God is the owner of everything.

© John Jonez 2024. All Rights Reserved.

Everything was created through him and for him. He existed before anything else, and he holds all creation together.

PAUL NOTES EVERYTHING IS TEMPORARY

1 Timothy 6:7 (NIV)
For we brought nothing into the world, and we can take nothing out of it.

Do we believe we own the things we have because we "earned" them? Scripture tells us otherwise:

Deuteronomy 8:18 (NIV)
But remember the Lord you God, for it is He who gives you the ability to produce wealth.

So then, we can come to the following conclusions:

1. God owns everything.
2. All we have has been *loaned* to us by God; it is not *owned* by us.
3. All we have is God's to *own*, and ours to *manage* on His behalf.

SCRIPTURE IS ALSO CLEAR: WE ARE HIS MANAGERS

God chose Adam to be the manager, not the owner:

Genesis 2:15 (NIV)
The Lord God took the man and put him in the Garden of Eden to work it and take care of it.

God chose all of us, individually and together, to carry out His plan:

Ephesians 2:10 (NIV)
For we are God's handiwork, created in Christ Jesus to do good works, which God prepared in advance for us to do.

WHAT DOES GOD EXPECT OF A MANAGER (STEWARD)?

Stewardship (Definition) – "the careful and responsible management of something entrusted to your care"[4]

Very few things in Scripture are stated more clearly than the expectations God has for a steward of His Creation. It is clear all of His followers are in fact expected to be stewards or managers of all we have been given, including every minute of every day we are on this planet.

1 Corinthians 4:2 (NLT)
Now a person who is put in charge as a manager must be FAITHFUL (emphasis added).

Luke 16:10 (NIV)
Whoever can be TRUSTED with very little can also be trusted with much, and whoever is dishonest with very little will also be dishonest with much (emphasis added).

What then, is our conclusion? A good steward is faithful to the owner, and trustworthy as a manager.

A good steward is faithful to the owner, and trustworthy as a manager.

FREE MARKET ECONOMY: PROPERTY OWNERSHIP IS FUNDAMENTAL

Although God makes it clear He owns everything, we live day-to-day in a Western economic system completely based upon property ownership. We cannot escape it, even if we wanted to. We can think of ownership as the "axle" around which the "wheel" of our economy spins. Every economic transaction involving a sale by one person or business, and a purchase by another, creates a transaction transferring ownership. For example:

- Home and property ownership—recorded by a Deed of Trust
- Vehicle ownership—recorded by a title
- Personal property ownership—a purchase and sales receipt

We spend a lifetime accumulating things we own, not things we manage, and we deal with some type of "ownership issue" nearly every day. Ownership can involve the simple purchase of a bottle of milk or a gallon of gas, or something far more complex such as a partnership agreement, mineral rights, or business ownership. Many of these require a written contract, often hundreds of pages, written by high-priced attorneys on both sides of the transaction. The courts of this country are filled with civil cases involving disputes about ownership.

© John Jonez 2024. All Rights Reserved.

So, is it inconsistent to point out, as followers of Christ, that *God* owns everything, while at the same time being completely immersed in a system of economics where *we* own everything? The answer is no, and Scripture can help us with this apparent dichotomy.

BELIEVERS IN CHRIST HAVE "DUAL CITIZENSHIP"

As human beings, we are citizens of our temporary home on Earth. At the same time, Paul tells us that, as believers, we are citizens of our true home in Heaven. In John's Gospel, Jesus makes it clear that His Kingdom is not "of this world," and He is not "of this world." For those who have put their faith in Christ, they are counted as children of God, and one day will be with Him in Heaven.

On a practical level, we will always deal with "ownership" during this lifetime, but even while on Earth we must have the perspective that we are not of this world. Our attitude and behavior must reflect the truth that God owns everything, and we are to manage all He has entrusted to us. The good news is that Scripture gives us amazing insights on how to live our lives focused on His ownership of all we have.

Philippians 3:20 (NLT)
But we are citizens of heaven, where the Lord Jesus Christ lives. And we are eagerly waiting for him to return as our Savior.

John 18:36a (NIV)
Jesus said, *"My kingdom is not of this world…"*

John 8:23 (NLT)
Jesus continued, *"You are from below; I am from above. You belong to this world; I do not."*

Ephesians 2:6 (NIV)
And God raised us up with Christ and seated us with him in the heavenly realms in Christ Jesus,

AMERICAN CULTURE—"THE AMERICAN DREAM"

The American Dream (Traditional "Aspirational" Definition) – "That dream of a land in which life should be better and richer and fuller for everyone, with opportunity for each according to ability or achievement." [5]

This traditional definition was created in 1931 during the Great Depression by James Truslow Adams, author of the book *The Epic of America*. Though the term has

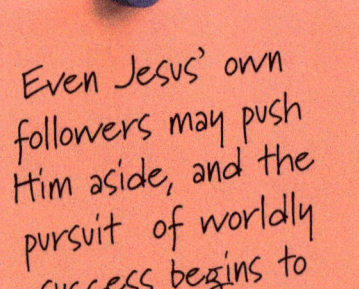

Even Jesus' own followers may push Him aside, and the pursuit of worldly success begins to take center stage.

The American Dream in the 1950s

had many definitions over time, the concept has its roots in the United States Declaration of Independence, which contains two key phrases: "all men are created equal," and the unalienable right to "life, liberty, and the pursuit of happiness."

Adams states: "It is not a dream of motor cars and high wages merely, but a dream of social order in which each man and each woman shall be able to attain the fullest stature of which they are innately capable, and be recognized by others for what they are, regardless of the fortuitous circumstances of birth or position."

The American Dream (Cultural "Corrupted" Definition) – "The idea that the pursuit of worldly success, money, wealth, and physical possessions will lead to fulfillment and happiness."

Our culture has evolved more recently to a corrupted view of the American Dream, focused on a pursuit of worldly success. For many people, this pursuit becomes the main focus of their life, guided by a cultural belief that money and possessions lead to happiness and fulfillment. Even for followers of Jesus, He may get pushed aside, and the pursuit begins to take center stage.

Culture has always had a powerful influence on its citizens, including Money. Trends, fads, or movements can get started and although they may be temporary, they can have a lasting impact on the thinking and behavior of people. Think of these cultural categories involving Money:

<u>**Yuppie**</u> **(1980s)** – "Young Urban Professional." Typically, these are wealthy people with good-paying jobs who are up-and-coming in their careers.

DINK (at the height of the Yuppie era) – "Double Income, No Kids." Viewed as having excess income often used to travel frequently and own "nicer" things.

DINKWAD – "Double Income, No Kids, With a Dog."

YOLO (early 1990s) – "You Only Live Once." An attitude of doing what you want, when you want, regardless of the cost.

FIRE (1990s–Present) – "Financially Independent, Retire Early." Marked by frugality and prioritizing the saving of money in order to retire young.

HENRY (early 2000s) – "High Earner, Not Rich Yet." This label did not catch on with the same popularity as the others, but it describes a person with the skills and drive to become wealthy.

HIFI (early 2000s–present) – "High Income, Financially Insecure." Describing a younger person, mostly Millennial or GenZ, with excessive spending focused on having fun, and keeping up with their friends. They are therefore financially unprepared for the future.

MONEY PRIORITIZATION IN WESTERN CULTURE (IN PRIORITY ORDER)[6]

1. Lifestyle Spending – #1 Priority!
2. Debt – Mortgages, student loans, credit cards, consumer debt
3. Savings – Often an afterthought
4. Giving – Usually the "leftovers"

For people in or near poverty, where life-or-death survival may be at risk the focus is on simply trying to stay alive. So, for them, the money priorities shown above are not relevant. The issues surrounding extreme poverty are beyond the scope of this study.

For most people in Western countries, spending on a desired lifestyle is their first priority. In economies largely driven by consumer spending, where people are bombarded daily with highly effective marketing, our real *needs* are satisfied fairly quickly, but our *wants* are often unlimited. Because *wants* often exceed our income, purchases using consumer debt has become normal and expected, especially for those just leaving their parents' home and beginning a life on their own.

Historically, the purchase of a home, with a mortgage, has been a good investment as long as it is well within one's ability to afford. Saving enough money to buy a first home without a mortgage is virtually impossible for most people, as their savings accumulation would simply chase, but never catch up to, the ever-increasing price of a home.

Beyond a mortgage, most debt is focused on increasing a desired lifestyle before the ability to pay cash for the purchase. So, we should think of this type of debt as "premature spending," that is, spending by borrowing and making future payments.

This is an issue for lower, middle, and upper-middle incomes alike. It is also an issue for believers and non-believers.

> Lifestyle spending by the Relentless Pursuer is often impulsive and frivolous, where all "wants" are viewed as "needs" without differentiation.

THE EXTREME CASE OF THE RELENTLESS PURSUER

A specific case we can characterize as the "Relentless Pursuer" is one where lifestyle spending is truly extreme compared to a person's level of wealth. They reach for a lifestyle beyond what they can actually afford. The *appearance* of wealth greater than their actual wealth is critically important to them. This person usually has at least a middle-class or upper-middle-class income where all the basic needs of life are met. Their spending is well above what would be considered prudent at their income level.

Lifestyle spending by the Relentless Pursuer is often impulsive and frivolous, where all "wants" are viewed as "needs" without differentiation. Enough is never enough. An attitude of entitlement to have everything they want is usually present: "I deserve it." Because the desire for things well exceeds their income, large amounts of debt are used

© John Jonez 2024. All Rights Reserved.

> "...and the people bowed and prayed to the neon god they made."
>
> "The Sound of Silence," Simon and Garfunkel, 1964

to fund purchases. The focus is on the monthly payment, rather than the actual price of any item. The situation can result in choosing which bills to pay in any given month because funds are insufficient to pay them all.

Note, these same characteristics may be present for some in the very-rich or ultra-rich class, but the difference is these people have enough wealth to buy everything they will ever want.

John D. Rockefeller, the world's first billionaire, believed to be the richest man who ever lived (adjusted for inflation), answered the question, "How much is enough?" by replying, "Just a little bit more!" If they were honest with themselves, many people would answer this question the same way.

In 1964, Paul Simon of Simon and Garfunkel wrote the song "The Sound of Silence." The lyrics in this song are very dark, portraying the incredible loneliness of many people and their inability to connect with others. Included in those lyrics are these words: "…and the people bowed and prayed to the neon god they made." How accurately descriptive of our culture are these words to this day.

Scripture warns of the futility of this pursuit, in the simplest possible words:

Ecclesiastes 5:10 (NIV)
Whoever loves money never has enough; whoever loves wealth is never satisfied with their income. This too is meaningless.

For followers of Christ, regarding today's culture, Paul warns us:

Colossians 2:8 (NIV)
See to it that no one takes you captive through hollow and deceptive philosophy, which depends on human tradition and the elemental spiritual forces of this world rather than on Christ.

A person following anything or anyone other than Jesus Himself is described by Scripture:

Romans 1:25 (NIV)
They exchanged the truth about God for a lie, and worshiped and served created things rather than the Creator—who is forever praised.

MONEY, WEALTH, AND POSSESSIONS—DO THEY LEAD TO HAPPINESS?

The point of emphasis in this section is not that God's purpose for our life is to make us *happy*—but rather His desire is to make us *holy*. He is worthy of our faithfulness to Him in any and all circumstances, and our relentless pursuit of Him alone will lead to fulfillment surpassing any other pursuit on planet Earth.

$$\$ = \odot\, ?$$

THE LIFE EXPERIENCE FROM AN EXPERT

Jessie O'Neill, author of the book *The Golden Ghetto: The Psychology of Affluence*, has particular expertise on this topic. "The Golden Ghetto" describes the environment inhabited by millions of Americans and their families who embrace and endlessly pursue the fantasy that "more is better." [7]

O'Neill grew up in a very wealthy family as the granddaughter of Charles E. Wilson, CEO of General Motors, who became Secretary of Defense in 1953 under President Eisenhower. At a fairly young age, she inherited substantial wealth. At age 40, she became a psychotherapist with a professional practice focused exclusively on treating the problems of those who had amassed great wealth or inherited great wealth—both the wealthy and the children of the wealthy.

> "Whoever loves money never has enough."
> Ecclesiastes 5:10

Speaking from her personal experiences, and her years in private practice, O'Neill concluded the following:

- Wealth creates a false sense of entitlement, and inherited wealth most often damages self-esteem, self-worth, and confidence.
- In an affluent family, because everything is immediate, inherited wealth results in an inability to:
    » handle delayed gratification
    » control impulses
    » effectively manage disappointment and frustration

O'Neill concluded, "When we learn to value ourselves simply for who we are, to love our children simply because they are our children, and radically shift our priorities and focus our energies and resources on helping those less fortunate than we are, we will be on our way to create a new American Dream."

See Appendix E for a full review of Jessie O'Neill's book, *The Golden Ghetto*.

A STUDY IN SECULAR PSYCHOLOGY

In his book, *The Two Most Important Days*, author Dr. Sanjiv Chopra, MD/PhD of the Harvard Medical School introduces the concept of "Hedonic Adaptation." The word "Hedonic" means "pertaining to pleasure," and the word "Adaptation" means "to adjust to." The concept, based on his studies, is that each person has an a built-in "baseline" level of happiness, which can be temporarily moved up or down by a joyous or sad event in life, but over time the person returns to his or her pre-set baseline.[8]

Here is an example of Hedonic Adaptation: a person has dreamed for years about someday purchasing a certain car, and the day they finally get it, it is absolutely *perfect*. The joyous event has moved his or her level of happiness much higher. In six months or so, the same car becomes a *nice* car, and the level of happiness is beginning to reset. A year later, the car becomes *normal*, and the level of happiness is back at its baseline. Sometime after that, in search of another joyous event, the person begins looking at the new model.

Dr. Chopra concludes that three things lead to the highest level of happiness and fulfillment:

1. Having purpose in life
2. Giving to others—both giving of ourselves and financial giving
3. Expressing gratitude—this may add 10 years to life expectancy

Note that these examples, and numerous other studies in secular psychology, conclude exactly what Scripture tells us: the *relentless pursuit* of "things," in an attempt to find happiness and fulfillment, is fruitless. Why? Because God created us for what Dr. Chopra concluded (above): purpose, giving, and gratitude!

THE "RELENTLESS PURSUIT" AND ITS DEVASTATING RESULTS

The following are some statistics regarding the population in America. In the richest country in the history of the world, it may seem impossible for these to be true, but they are:

- A recent Capital One Credit Wise survey revealed that 73% of respondents stated that Money is the number one source of their anxiety and stress.[9]
- Rich and poor both suffer stress.[10]
    - » Poor—stress about the obstacles and difficulties of daily life
    - » Rich—stress about maintaining lifestyle and appearance of wealth to others
- As of 2023, 96% of Americans are concerned about the state of the economy.[11]
- 46% of Americans, age 60–64, have less than $1000 saved for retirement.[12]
- 63% of Americans have enough savings to cover a $400 emergency. This peaked in 2021 at 68%, from a low of 50% in 2013.[13]
- 36% of Americans have no room in their garage to park a car![14]

© John Jonez 2024. All Rights Reserved.

DISCOVERING AND DEMOLISHING STRONGHOLDS

STRONGHOLD: EXCESSIVE FOCUS ON MONEY AND POSSESSIONS

This stronghold can present itself in several ways, starting with money being a simple "distraction" in our life. But at the extreme, our life may fit the definition of the "Relentless Pursuer." This "Excessive Focus," at whatever level it exists in our life, is certain to begin eroding God's design to "seek Him first" at all times. Money and possessions will come first and everything else becomes secondary.

An excessive focus on money and possessions may have at its core an exaggerated self-ambition to succeed, a sense of entitlement, or pride. Or, it may simply be a lack of understanding of God's truth about money. In virtually every case it creates a scarcity of contentment in our attitude towards God's provision. Although it may be counter intuitive, this stronghold can manifest itself in a wide range of income levels. Unfortunately, it also carries a high level of anxiety.

DIAGNOSTIC STATEMENTS

Consider the following statements, checking each one as it applies to you and your thinking, to help identify whether an "Excessive Focus" has had an influence in your life:

- ❏ My work is the highest priority in my life.
- ❏ Making more money is the most important reason I work so hard.
- ❏ Taking care of my possessions consumes a significant portion of my free time.
- ❏ I grew up with very little, and I'm making up for it now.
- ❏ I am envious of other people when they have nicer things than I do.
- ❏ I often compare myself to others to make sure I "measure up."
- ❏ I am independent and "self-made."
- ❏ I am secretly motivated to be more successful than my coworkers and neighbors.
- ❏ When I get new things, my favorite part is showing them off to other people.
- ❏ My title at work is extremely important; to some extent, it defines who I am.
- ❏ The pressure I feel to provide nice things for my family is extremely high, and it all rests on my shoulders.
- ❏ I am more important and more significant because of what I have.
- ❏ I count every penny because "it's all up to me" to "make it."
- ❏ I own my stuff. The idea that God owns everything is hard for me to grasp.
- ❏ I have my own expectation of a standard of living for my family.
- ❏ I work hard for all that I have, so therefore I am entitled to have it.
- ❏ I'm not poor, but I constantly struggle to make ends meet.
- ❏ Giving money away is really hard for me—after all, I earned it.
- ❏ Having a secure financial future is equally important as having nice things.
- ❏ If I am honest with myself, deep down I want people to view me as wealthy.
- ❏ The money and things I have are fine, but I'll always want more.

SPIRITUAL TRANSACTION FOR "EXCESSIVE FOCUS" USING THE 4RS PRAYER MODEL:

1. REPENT – Turn away from the "Excessive Focus" on money and turn toward God as the highest priority in your life.

Sample Prayer – Father, I acknowledge I have placed money and possessions as an excessively high priority in my life. That pursuit has caused You, my Creator, to be moved out of first place. Forgive me now for my choice to focus on money ahead of You in my heart, my life, and my schedule. I ask for forgiveness for my attitude of entitlement, for my overzealous work life, my worry that I won't have enough, and my lack of contentment with what You choose to provide. I recognize this as sin, and commit to creating more balanced patterns in my life.

2. REBUKE – Rebuke Mammon and every other evil spirit influencing this area of your life.

Sample Prayer – In Jesus' powerful name, I rebuke Mammon and every evil spirit in my life that has distracted me and caused this Excessive Focus on money. I renounce the lies that money leads to fulfillment, to happiness, or that I won't have enough, and that "more" is always better. By the authority of Jesus, I command these spirits to leave my thinking, my behavior, and every influence on my family.

3. REPLACE – Replace every lie or false thought with God's truth.

Sample Prayer – Father, I replace every lie and falsehood with Your truth. I agree with Your truth that I am significant just because I am Your child, loved exactly as I am created, and created to put You first in everything I do.

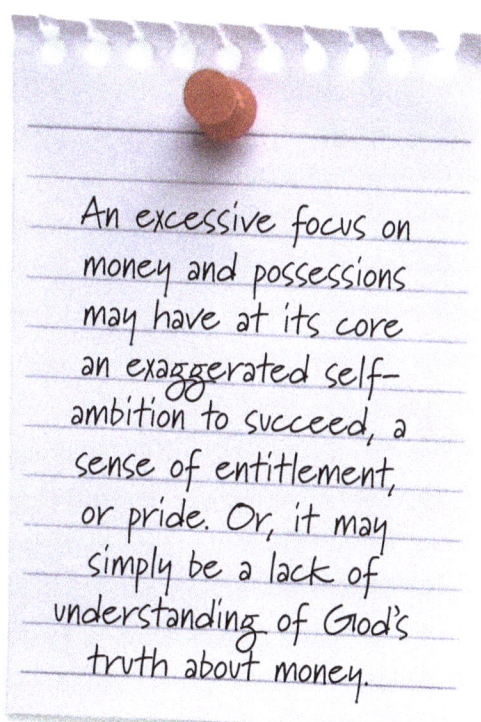

An excessive focus on money and possessions may have at its core an exaggerated self-ambition to succeed, a sense of entitlement, or pride. Or, it may simply be a lack of understanding of God's truth about money.

© John Jonez 2024. All Rights Reserved.

4. <u>RECEIVE</u> – Receive the Lord's promise of forgiveness, His truth, and a fresh infilling of the Holy Spirit.

Sample Prayer – Father, thank You for the gift and promise of forgiveness. I receive that gift with utmost gratitude and humility. Fill me with Your Holy Spirit in every place in my heart, mind, and spirit that was occupied by the sinful "Excessive Focus" on money. I receive the peace and joy right now that comes with faithfulness to You and Your Word. In Jesus' Name, Amen

RELATED SCRIPTURES

James 3:16 (NIV)
For where you have envy and selfish ambition, there you find disorder and every evil practice.

Matthew 16:24 (NIV)
Then Jesus said to his disciples, "Whoever wants to be my disciple must deny themselves and take up their cross and follow me."

Romans 12:2 (NIV)
Do not conform to the pattern of this world, but be transformed by the renewing of your mind. Then you will be able to test and approve what God's will is—his good, pleasing and perfect will.

1 Timothy 6:6 (NIV)
But godliness with contentment is great gain.

PRACTICAL APPLICATION – WALKING IN THE OPPOSITE DIRECTION

- ☐ I will proactively review my life's priorities, and make decisions to reorder those priorities to be in alignment with God's truths and His design for my life.

- ☐ I will proactively seek to understand and fully internalize my exclusive identity as a child of God through faith in Christ.

- ☐ I will replace the importance I have placed on wanting people view me as wealthy, successful, and independent with a singular importance focused on how God views me.

- ☐ I will review the priorities I have historically placed on money as "lifestyle spending" first, and prioritize "giving" first.

- ☐ I will replace the view of myself as the *owner* of all I have with viewing myself as a *manager* of all that God has entrusted to me.

- ☐ Each day, I will acknowledge that my provision, in whatever amount it is, comes from God alone.

A calm and modest life brings more happiness than the pursuit of success combined with constant restlessness.

— Albert Einstein, 1922

SECTION FOUR
Giving Is an Act of Worship

Notes: _____

In this section, the focus is specifically about giving and its relationship to our worship of God. We will most likely see a reordering of priorities in our lives, and how it leads to our own spiritual growth. A thorough examination of giving requires an examination in multiple dimensions.

Worship (Definition) – "To honor, obey, and emulate Jesus by how we live"

This definition is intentionally broad for our purpose in this chapter. Our external actions should become more and more like Jesus throughout our lives, as confirmation of the transformation taking place in our hearts. Every time we give to others or are faithful to Him in any way, it is a form of worship.

THE REORDERING OF MONEY PRIORITIZATION

Recall from Section 2, most Western Cultures prioritize money as follows:

1. Lifestyle Spending – #1 priority!
2. Debt – Mortgages, student loans, credit cards, consumer debt
3. Savings – Often an afterthought
4. Giving – Usually the "leftovers"

God's design for money priorities, exactly the opposite of what is shown above:[15]

1. Giving – Our highest priority, because we are grateful
2. Saving – There is wisdom in saving.
3. Debt – It is dangerous, and comes with a cautionary warning.
4. Lifestyle spending – Last priority. Contentment is a virtue.

This order demonstrates our focus on giving to God by giving to others as our first priority, wisely saving for the future, being cautious about debt, and funding our own lifestyle last with what is left over.

Why would God want us to prioritize giving as our first priority?

Proverbs 3:9–10 (NIV)
Honor the Lord with your wealth, with the firstfruits of all your crops; then your barns will be filled to overflowing, and your vats will brim over with new wine.

In Proverbs, we see the wisdom of honoring the Lord with our "firstfruits." In the agricultural economy of that time period, owning land and raising animals or growing crops was a common source of wealth. The "firstfruits" gift is a specific kind of gift with specific parameters, presented to the Levite priests on various occasions. The point here is not the specific type of gift, but the *priority* of that gift. It is to be given first. It is one of many examples in Scripture we should follow to give *first*, and make giving our highest priority.

In Matthew 6, using examples of food and clothing, Jesus tells His followers to seek His Kingdom and righteousness *first*, as they are more important than anything else, then these other things will be given.

Matthew 6:33 (NIV)
But seek first his kingdom and his righteousness, and all these things will be given to you as well.

We should view giving as our act of worship, our demonstration of surrender to God, and giving should come first. Remember, He owns it all.

There are four dimensions of giving, three of which we will examine carefully in this chapter:

A. Giving is God's **original design** for His people.
B. Giving requires our **faith**.

> God's priorities for His money are the exact opposite of what the culture tells us.

© John Jonez 2024. All Rights Reserved.

C. Giving requires a choice of our **will**.

D. Giving generously requires our _____ (wait until the next chapter!)

GIVING IS GOD'S ORIGINAL DESIGN FOR HIS PEOPLE

Genesis 1:27 (NIV)
So, God created mankind in his own image, in the image of God he created them; male and female he created them.

John 3:16 (NIV)
For God so loved the world that he gave his one and only Son, that whoever believes in him shall not perish but have eternal life.

In Genesis chapter one, we learn that we are made in *His own image.* Of course this doesn't mean we *look* like God, but we are made to be like Him *in character.* It is something we spend a lifetime on Earth striving to achieve—to live our lives emulating Jesus.

We also know that God gave the world the greatest Gift ever given, His Son Jesus, that we may be reconciled to the Father, with our broken relationship now healed and restored. Since we are made in His image, and He is a generous giver, then it is easy to conclude we are to give also. These two truths of Scripture are easily connected.

2 Corinthians 9:15 (NIV)
*Thanks be to God for his **indescribable** gift.*

Other translations of this verse:
(ESV) *Thanks be to God for his **inexpressible** gift!*
(NLT) *Thank God for this gift **too wonderful for words**!*

In these verses, God's gift of Jesus is characterized as "indescribable," "inexpressible," and "too wonderful for words." Don't we understand the highest value of anything can be described as "priceless"? The gift to all humanity of His Son Jesus is truly priceless, isn't it? How can it be "indescribable"?

The word "priceless" has two parts to its full meaning. The first component of something considered "priceless" is that the person who possesses it will not part with it under any circumstance. The second part is that no one could come up with enough money or a great enough promise to convince the holder of the "priceless" item to

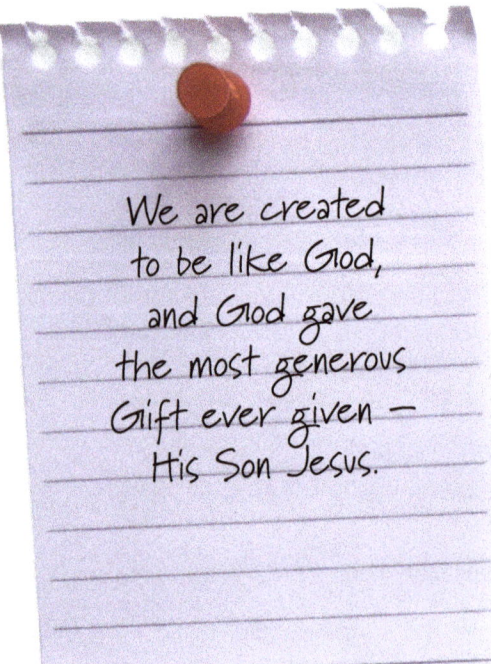

We are created to be like God, and God gave the most generous Gift ever given — His Son Jesus.

© John Jonez 2024. All Rights Reserved.

let go it. The clearest example to any parent is the value of their children—truly priceless!

But in the case of God's gift of Jesus, God chose to give His Son away—for us! Therefore, it doesn't fit the definition of "priceless," and there are no words in any language to describe this act of giving or the value of the gift. It is *greater than* priceless, and that's why it is "indescribable," "inexpressible," and "too wonderful for words." Let that sink in—something of such great value for which we literally have no words to describe!

Let us conclude: because of His indescribable gift to us, our gratitude should be immeasurable. Are we grateful *enough*?

GIVING REQUIRES OUR FAITH, AND OUR FAITH REQUIRES GIVING

This diagram shows and describes the relationship between faith, hope, and righteousness. The very first act of our faith is to *confess* our sins, *believe* in our heart that Jesus died and God raised Him from the dead, place our *trust* in Jesus, and *receive* Him as our Lord and Savior (Romans 10:9). It is our first and most important *spiritual transaction.* This act of faith begins the lifelong journey of following Him and walking in a restored relationship with God the Father, a gift only available through Jesus (John 14:6).

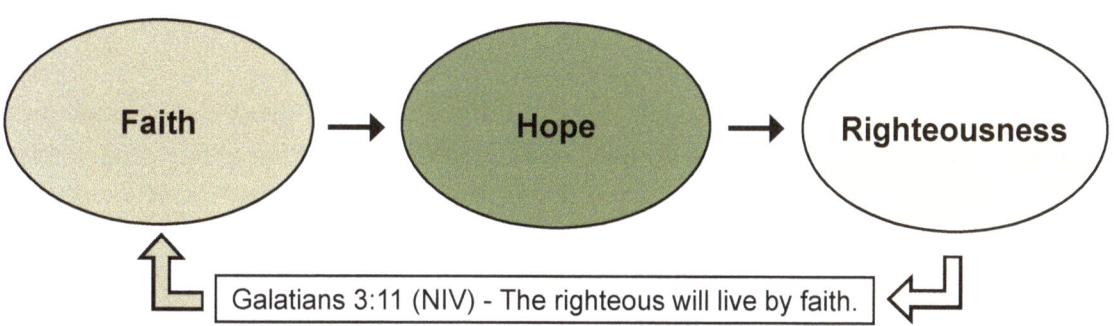

Hebrews 11:1 (NIV) - Faith is being sure of what we hope for, and certain of what we do not see.

1. How do we demonstrate we are sure?
   - James 2:18 (NIV) - I will show you my faith by what I do.
2. What is that we hope for?
   - "Righteousness" (Galatians 5:5)

Galatians 5:5 (NIV) - But by faith we eagerly await, through the Spirit, the righteousness for which we hope.

Righteousness: Being made right in the eyes of God - immediate and ongoing.

Philippians 3:9 (NLT) - I become righteous through faith in Christ. (Justification)

1 Timothy 6:11 (NLT) - Pursue righteousness and a godly life. (Sanctification)

© John Jonez 2024. All Rights Reserved.

At that very moment we receive salvation, we become a new creation (2 Corinthians 5:17), receive the Holy Spirit (Acts 1:8), and are declared righteous before God (Philippians 3:9). And, as the Apostle Paul pointed out in Galatians 3:11 (quoting Habakkuk 2:4): "The righteous shall live by faith."

WHAT IS FAITH?

Faith (Definition) – "A belief not based on proof. Confidence in a person or thing."[16]

Scripture provides a concise definition:

Hebrews 11:1 (NIV)
Now faith is being sure of what we hope for, and certain of what we do not see.

1. How do we demonstrate we are sure of something?
If we are sure of something, or at least as sure as we possibly can be, we no longer question it, but we *act* on it. By way of analogy, a clear example of "being sure" can be seen by answering this question: "How does the parachutist demonstrate he is sure the parachute will open when he jumps out of the airplane?" He can ask all the questions in advance about how well it was packed, how old it is, if this type of parachute is reliable, and so on. But the only way to demonstrate he is sure by his *action* is to jump! No other action will demonstrate his faith in the parachute as completely as this—no more words, just action.

So it is with our faith: demonstrating our faith requires action. We don't have the luxury of seeing Jesus or seeing God with our own eyes. But once again, Scripture shows us how to demonstrate the *sureness* of our faith: we *act*.

1 Peter 1:8 (NIV)
Though you have not seen him, you love him; and even though you do not see him now, you believe in him.

James 2:18 (NIV)
I will show you my faith by what I do.

We can conclude, just like the parachutist, that demonstrating and living out our faith requires *action*.

2. What is it we hope for?

As believers, we hope for many things, but there is one specific thing that should occupy the place of hope in us above all—the declaration of our righteousness through faith in Jesus—which happens the moment we place our faith in Him. We cannot earn this on our own; it only comes by faith in Jesus' saving work on our behalf. We are made righteous in God's eyes because of Jesus' righteousness imparted to us.

Galatians 5:5 (NIV)
But by faith, we eagerly await through the Spirit, the righteousness for which we hope.

3. What is righteousness?

We define "righteousness" as "being right with God." Note that righteousness has two parts: one is *immediate* and the other is *ongoing*. In Paul's letter to the Philippians, we learn there is a declaration of righteousness for believers who put their faith in Christ, and it is part of the original spiritual transaction of salvation. This is the first part of righteousness we call "justification." An easy way to remember this word and its meaning is this: when a person places their faith in Christ, it is "just as if they never sinned," because they are forgiven at that moment.

Philippians 3:9 (NLT)
I become righteous through faith in Christ. (Justification)

The second part of righteousness is shown in 1 Timothy when Paul tells Timothy to "pursue righteousness and a godly life." What Paul is telling Timothy is to flee from the things of this world that bring harm, and to pursue the good things of God that give life. As believers are set apart from this world to do the work of God, we call this "sanctification."

1 Timothy 6:11 (NLT)
Pursue righteousness and a godly life. (Sanctification)

> By faith, we eagerly await, the Righteousness for which we hope — which comes from no other King than Jesus Christ.

We can think of these two parts of righteousness as the two components in the process of making Jesus our Lord and Savior. Making Him our Savior happens immediately when we place our faith in Him. At that moment, our salvation for eternity is secure. However, making Him Lord— the one Master of our life, and becoming more and more like Him—is an ongoing process—one that will continue for the rest of our lives. Though we are declared righteous once, we are to pursue righteousness on an ongoing basis; as righteous people we are required to live *by faith.*

Galatians 3:11 (NIV)
The righteous will live by faith.

Note the circular nature of the relationship between faith, hope, and righteousness. We start by placing our faith in Christ. Our faith requires us to take action demonstrating the certainty of our faith and our active hope in the righteousness of Jesus. The more we pursue righteousness, the stronger our faith becomes, the deeper our hope, and on and on. As this process of spiritual maturing manifests itself externally in our actions, transformation of our hearts occurs.

What does all this have to do with our giving? The title of this section is "Giving Is an Act of Worship"; notice that word "act." Earlier, we defined worship as "to honor, obey, and emulate Jesus by how we live." To do this, we "pursue righteousness" for the rest of our lives. Part of this pursuit is coming to terms with the influence of Mammon in our lives, and our relationship with Money. Pursuing righteousness requires action, one of which is giving. Giving requires our faith; and our faith requires giving.

Proverbs 3:9 (NLT)
Honor the Lord with your wealth and with the best part of everything you produce.

GIVING REQUIRES OUR WILL

This next dimension of giving is the one involving our will. It is important to remember this is one, *and only one*, of the four dimensions. If this were the only dimension to giving, then we would always choose to give only because we *force* ourselves to do so. This singular dimension would not engage the heart, and we would miss all that God truly wants for us in this area of our lives. Yet, the dimension of our "will" is important.

Will (Definition) – "The faculty of conscious and deliberate action, the act or process of asserting one's choice. A determination, decision, or resolution."[17]

It is certainly true, if we decide to give in a meaningful way, that we must follow through and do it—deliberately, consistently and with conviction. That is what it means to give as an intentional act of our will.

Alternatively, if we choose to give only when we feel like it, by only responding to our emotions, then our actions will become erratic and inconsistent. Imagine if we did things in life only when we felt like it, rather than consistently and with determined intention. How would that work out in our marriage? Would we ever finish school? What would happen if we only showed up to work when we felt like it? Or what if we drove on the highway in whatever way we felt like at the moment, rather than following the rules of the road? None of these scenarios would produce good results.

Scripture tells us we are to be consistent, deliberate, and disciplined in our actions.

Deuteronomy 11:1 (NIV)
Love the Lord your God and keep his requirements, his decrees, his law and his commands always.

John 14:15 (NIV)
If you love me, keep my commands.

These verses are unmistakably black and white. They do not say "sometimes," or "when we feel like it"—they clearly say or imply *always*. Our giving must be a consistent action based on our will, not an erratic behavior driven by our emotions.

© John Jonez 2024. All Rights Reserved.

> Every time I give, it reminds me that God owns everything, and I'm grateful for all He has entrusted to me.

There is a huge benefit for us when our giving is done consistently. By way of analogy, consider how we participate in Communion on a weekly or monthly basis. Jesus commanded us to take Communion "in remembrance of Me." If we are active and consistent in Scripture reading and prayer time, we remember Him every day, most likely several times each day. But when we take Communion, there is a deeper reflection and often emotional moment of remembering specifically what He did for us. The bread and wine signify His sacrifice on the cross, and we are to be grateful for that.

A consistent pattern of giving can have a similar effect on us. Though we remember Him every day, by giving each week or month it serves as a frequent reminder that God owns everything, and we are to manage His money His way. Each time we give, we should express our gratitude as He provides for our every need.

THE CONTRAST OF TWO CHARACTERS

Character #1:

Luke 18:18-23 (NIV)—The Rich Young Ruler

"A certain ruler asked him, "Good teacher, what must I do to inherit eternal life?"

"Why do you call me good?" Jesus answered. *"No one is good—except God alone. You know the commandments: 'Do not commit adultery, do not murder, do not steal, do not give false testimony, honor your father and mother.'"*

"All these I have kept since I was a boy," he said.

When Jesus heard this, he said to him, *"You still lack one thing. Sell everything you have and give to the poor, and you will have treasure in heaven. Then come, follow me."*

"When he heard this, he became very sad, because he was a man of great wealth."

Scripture does not tell us the end of this story. We do not know if the ruler eventually did what Jesus told him to do. Scripture only states he was very sad because of his great wealth, so maybe he thought about it and did it later. Judging by his reaction to what Jesus said, it is clear his wealth was the most important thing to him. We can conclude Mammon had influenced him, and the ruler may not have even been aware of the source of influence.

The real point of this story is for all of us to ensure we choose God as our master, above all else, including Mammon.

Character #2

The Sayings of Agur, Son of Jakeh—Proverbs 30.

As declared to Ithiel, and Ucal. Very little is known about these four characters, but Agur has the entire chapter devoted to his wisdom.

Here are the words of Agur:

Proverbs 30:7–9 (NLT)
"O God, I beg two favors from you; let me have them before I die.
First, help me never to tell a lie.
Second, give me neither poverty nor riches!
Give me just enough to satisfy my needs.
For if I grow rich, I may deny you and say, 'Who is the Lord?'
And if I am too poor, I may steal and thus insult God's holy name."

Agur was sharing his heart with God, wanting to live his life for Him without distractions. He understood the temptations of riches, and the challenges of poverty, asking God to supply him with just enough for his needs. That sounds similar to the Lord's Prayer: "Give us this day, our daily bread".

Agur knew that if he grew rich, the riches might become the center of his life, pushing God from the center, and causing him to wonder if he would still need God at all. He also recognized that in poverty, he might be tempted to steal to satisfy his basic needs, breaking one of the ten commandments and thereby insulting God's holy name.

May each of us become as wise as Agur.

© John Jonez 2024. All Rights Reserved.

SECTION FIVE
Generosity: The Evidence of a Grateful Heart

The title of this section is our definition of generosity. The external actions of a follower of Jesus provide useful evidence regarding the condition of a person's heart. A lifestyle of giving generously is an indication of someone who is grateful for all God has done for them in the finished work of Jesus on the cross. The source and motivation of all true generosity is gratitude, and gratitude leads to a transformed heart. The word "gratitude" comes from two words: "grateful" and "attitude."

In Section IV we covered three of the four dimensions of giving:

A. Giving is God's *original design* for His people.
B. Giving requires our *faith*.
C. Giving requires our *will*.

In this section, we will explore the fourth dimension:

D. Giving generously requires our **heart**.

We will use the text in 2 Corinthians chapters 8 and 9 to deeply explore what a grateful and generous heart looks like, and the difference a generous person can make. In these two chapters, God demonstrates

His generosity to us as an example for us to imitate in our generosity towards others.

Focus especially on the following key verses from these chapters:

2 Corinthians 8:9 (NIV)
For you know the grace of our Lord Jesus Christ, that though he was rich, yet for your sakes he become poor, so that you through his poverty might become rich.

This verse is not about money. It says Jesus was "rich," yet there are no references in Scripture of Him having substantial material wealth. We are unaware if He ever owned a home, and we do not generally think of Him as being wealthy. The riches of Jesus are spiritual. They include grace, as mentioned in the first part of this verse, along with mercy, and the riches associated with the heavenly glory and fellowship He always and eternally enjoys with the Father.

The verse goes on to say, "For your sakes He became poor," referring to how Jesus emptied Himself and took on the likeness of humanity as a servant (Philippians 2:7), and how He gave His life on the cross so that we may become rich. Our riches include those accompanying our becoming children of God and spending eternity with Him. 1 Peter describes this gift is a *priceless inheritance* that is kept in Heaven for each of us.

1 Peter 1:4 (NLT)
…and we have a priceless inheritance—an inheritance that is kept in heaven for you, pure and undefiled, beyond the reach of change and decay.

God demonstrates His generosity in the verse below. He is generous to us *so that* we can be generous to others. He will make us rich—in grace, in resources, in provision, in health, and blessings in *every* way, so that we can be generous to others.

2 Corinthians 9:11 (NIV)
You will be enriched in every way so that you can be generous on every occasion, and through us your generosity will result in thanksgiving to God.

SETTING THE STAGE

The following is some background to Paul's letter to the Corinthians:

Gratitude = Grateful + Attitude

© John Jonez 2024. All Rights Reserved.

Notes: _____

- Paul is in Macedonia on his third missionary journey while writing this letter.
- He is dealing with the collection of money for the poor believers in Jerusalem, an effort which had begun a year earlier.
- The previous year, the Corinthians were the first to desire to give, and to begin giving.
- Paul is boasting to the Macedonians about the eagerness of the Corinthians to begin giving.
- He points out that the Corinthian church did not complete their giving, while the Macedonians gave well beyond Paul's expectations.
- Paul makes it clear in this scripture that he is disappointed the Corinthians have not completed the giving they had previously committed to do.

2 Corinthians 8:1–12, 24 and 9:1–15

Before proceeding, read all of these verses. Paul has much to say to the Corinthian church about generous giving. He will describe what a grateful and generous heart looks like, then describes what a difference being generous makes in the world, in other people, and in ourselves.

WHAT ARE THE CHARACTERISTICS OF GIVING FROM A GRATEFUL AND GENEROUS HEART?

1. It is unrelated to income or wealth.
   (2 Corinthians 8:2)
2. Its starting point is obedience.
   (2 Corinthians 9:13)
3. It is always focused first toward the Lord, then toward others.
   (2 Corinthians 8:5)
4. It is grounded in gratitude for God's grace.
   (2 Corinthians 8:9)
5. It views generosity as a privilege.
   (2 Corinthians 8:4)
6. It gives generously, not grudgingly.
   (2 Corinthians 9:5)
7. It sows generously, not sparingly.
   (2 Corinthians 9:6)
8. It gives cheerfully, not reluctantly.
   (2 Corinthians 9:7)
9. It is deeply personal between us and God.
   (2 Corinthians 9:7)
10. It is a manifestation of God's "incredible gift" to us. (2 Corinthians 9:15)

These characteristics provide substantial external evidence of a person's internal heart condition.

COULD GOD EVER BE DISAPPOINTED WITH OUR GIVING?

True or False: You have likely heard it said, "The *amount* of the gift doesn't matter; it's all about the *heart*."

There is one type of gift for which this statement is true. If you have children, then you may have experienced the joy of your first-grade child bringing home a Valentine's Day card for Daddy. He or she made it in school earlier that day. It's pink and white and red, with hearts all over it, and a message that includes "I love you, Daddy," written in bright Crayola red. It's the most heartfelt gift you have received (since last year's Valentine's Day card, of course). The monetary value of the gift is zero, but the impact to Daddy's heart is amazing, and many hugs and words of love ensue. Daddy and child both experience each other's joy of giving and receiving. Yes, this gift is *all about the heart*.

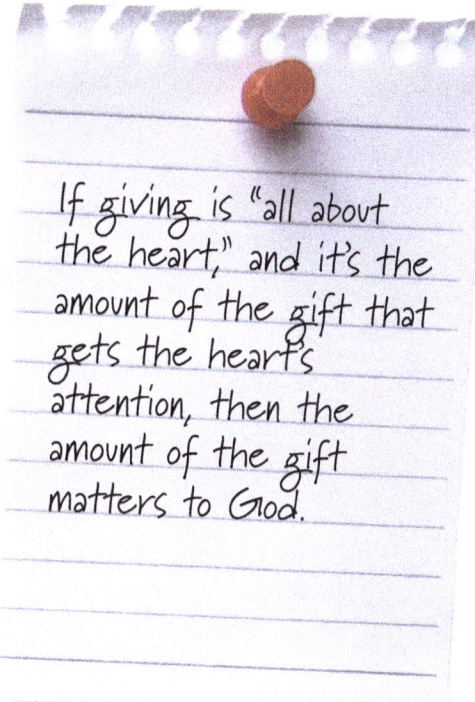

If giving is "all about the heart," and it's the amount of the gift that gets the heart's attention, then the amount of the gift matters to God.

But for the giving pattern of a follower of Jesus, the statement is false. When does a gift matter to God? Is God ever disappointed with our giving? Maybe He is pleased with every gift and He just wants us to be obedient and give *something*—a "check-the-box" exercise for us, and for God, that is surely good enough, right?

Maybe not. If giving is "all about the heart," and it's the *amount* of the gift that gets the heart's attention, then the amount of the gift matters to God. If the amount is so small that it really doesn't matter to us, then it has nothing to do with the heart.

We will explore this concept more using three stories in Scripture, looking for a pattern to God's (or Jesus') response to an act of giving.

CAIN AND ABEL'S GIFTS

Genesis 4:2b–5 (NLT)
When they grew up, Abel became a shepherd, while Cain cultivated the ground. When it was time for the harvest, Cain presented some of his crops as a gift to the Lord. Abel also brought a gift—the best portions of the firstborn lambs from his flock. The Lord accepted Abel and his gift, but he did not accept Cain and his gift. This made Cain very angry, and he looked dejected.

© John Jonez 2024. All Rights Reserved.

Cain's gift was not acceptable to God because it was just "some of his crops"; however, Abel's gift included the best portions of his firstborn lambs. Abel's gift was one of high value (the *amount*) and his *heart* was engaged in the gift. Cain's gift was of little value, and his heart was not engaged at all. Which gift mattered more to the giver, and therefore mattered more to God? Abel's gift, of course.

THE RICH PEOPLE AND THE WIDOW'S OFFERINGS IN THE TEMPLE

Luke 21:1–4 (NLT)
While Jesus was in the Temple, he watched the rich people dropping their gifts in the collection box. Then a poor widow came by and dropped in two small coins. "I tell you the truth," Jesus said, "this poor widow has given more than all the rest of them. For they have given a tiny part of their surplus, but she, poor as she is, has given everything she has."

The actual monetary value of the rich people's gift was greater than the widow's gift. The rich people's gift did not matter much to *them*, because they gave out of their excess, therefore it did not matter much to God either. But the widow gave nearly all she had, so the *amount* mattered greatly to her and it mattered greatly to God. The point Jesus made was that *relative* to what they each had, the widow's gift had greater *relative* value, because her heart was engaged in the act of giving.

ANANIAS, AND SAPPHIRA'S GIFT

Summary of Acts 5:1–10
Ananias and his wife Sapphira sold a piece of property and had previously committed to give all the proceeds to the apostles. But they held back part of the money for themselves, then lied about doing so. When Peter confronted Ananias about it, Ananias fell down and died. Later Peter asked Sapphira about it, and she also lied, unaware of what had just happened to her husband. Immediately she, too, fell down at Peter's feet and died.

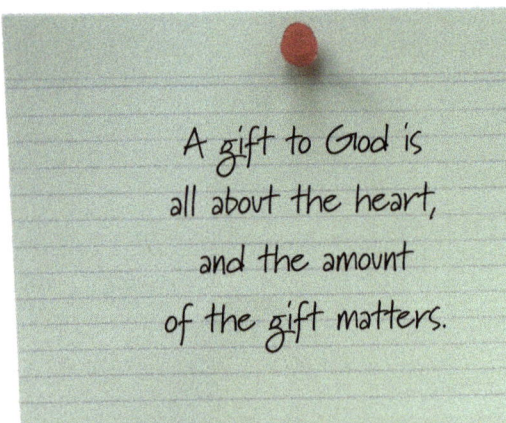

A gift to God is all about the heart, and the amount of the gift matters.

God shows His disappointment with Ananias and Sapphira. Satan had darkened their hearts and they paid the ultimate price for lying about their gift. Their gift was not acceptable to God.

In each of these three stories, we see with clarity: God *can* be disappointed with the giving of His people.

WHEN IS A GIFT ACCEPTABLE OR PLEASING TO GOD?

The story of Cain and Abel in Genesis 4 is the first example we see in Scripture of giving gifts. God used the word "acceptable" when evaluating Abel's gift, and He uses that term in other verses throughout the Bible on a variety of subjects.

We need to understand that the terms "acceptable" and "pleasing" are used throughout Scripture with identical meaning. In the English language, we might think of "acceptable" as "barely good enough," and "pleasing" to mean something *better than* acceptable. To see this in Scripture, consider the following familiar verse:

Psalm 19:14 (NLT)
May the words of my mouth and the meditation of my heart be pleasing to you, O Lord, my rock and my redeemer.

But numerous other translations use the word "acceptable" in place of "pleasing." We will consider these two terms to be synonymous as it relates to giving. Think of it this way: an *acceptable* gift to God is also a *pleasing* one to Him.

2 Corinthians 8:12 (NIV)
For if the willingness is there, the gift is acceptable according to what one has, not according to what he does not have.

2 Corinthians 9:7 (NIV)
Each man should give what he has decided in his heart to give, not reluctantly or under compulsion, for God loves a cheerful giver.

> "A man there was, and they called him mad; the more he gave, the more he had."
>
> — John Bunyan, Author, The Pilgrim's Progress

From these stories and scriptures, we can conclude several things about whether or not a gift is acceptable or pleasing to God:
- An amount that matters to us, matters to God.
- An amount that matters little to us, matters little to God.
- If it's "pocket change" to us, it's "pocket change" to God.
- The greater the amount, the greater the tug on our heart.
- It's the heart that makes the gift count; the money is just the tool God uses to capture our heart.

FOUR CHARACTERISTICS OF ACCEPTABLE AND PLEASING GIFTS TO GOD:[18]

1. The amount matters.
2. We determine the amount.
3. We give according to our ability. ("Proportional Giving")
4. The heart makes the gift count.

Following are some additional scriptures regarding acceptable and pleasing gifts:

Leviticus 1:3, 9b (NLT)
"If the animal you present as a burnt offering is from the herd, it must be a male with no defects. Bring it to the entrance of the Tabernacle so you may be accepted by the Lord. It is a special gift, a pleasing aroma to the Lord."

Philippians 4:18 (NLT)
At the moment I have all I need—and more! I am generously supplied with the gifts you sent me with Epaphroditus. They are a sweet-smelling sacrifice that is acceptable and pleasing to God.

Exodus 25:1–2 (NIV)
The Lord said to Moses, "Tell the Israelites to bring me an offering. You are to receive the offering for me from everyone whose heart prompts them to give."

WHAT IMPACT DOES A GENEROUS AND GRATEFUL PERSON MAKE FOR THEMSELVES AND OTHERS? (BASED ON 2 CORINTHIANS 8 AND 9)

1. Our generosity inspires generosity in others. (2 Corinthians 8:1–4)
2. Generosity honors the Lord. (2 Corinthians 8:19)
3. God receives thanksgiving from our giving. (2 Corinthians 9:11–12)
4. Generosity meets the practical needs of others. (2 Corinthians 8:14)

5. Generous givers demonstrate their sincere love for God and others. (2 Corinthians 8:8)
6. Others will praise God for your service and giving. (2 Corinthians 9:13)
7. We become more cheerful. (2 Corinthians 9:7)
8. In all things, and at all times, you will be rich in God's grace. (2 Corinthians 9:8)
9. You will abound in every good work. (2 Corinthians 9:8)
10. God will supply the seed, then increase the supply of seed, to continue sowing. (2 Corinthians 9:10)
11. God will provide bread to eat. (2 Corinthians 9:10)
12. You will experience an enlarged harvest of righteousness, becoming more like Jesus. (2 Corinthians 9:10)
13. The grateful and generous giver will be made rich in every way—for this purpose—so they can be generous at all times. (2 Corinthians 9:11)

You see, generosity is about what God wants for us, not what He wants from us.

The grateful and generous giver can make a tremendously positive impact for God's Kingdom, for other people, and for themselves. But the development of a grateful heart, resulting in generous giving, is a journey. Not everyone is a grateful and generous giver, at least not yet.

CONSIDER THESE FOUR TYPES OF GIVERS:

1. Non-Giver – Just what it sounds like
2. Reluctant Giver – Occasional giving out of obligation
3. Obedient Giver – Routine giving based on their "will" but not their heart
4. Grateful Giver – All about the heart
   » Giving is motivated purely out of gratitude for God's "indescribable" gift.
   » Generosity is viewed as a path to a more intimate relationship with God.
   » Generous giving reflects a surrendered and transformed heart.
   » This giver is generous at all times, and in all things.
   » Generous giving brings joy to the heart.

The **Non-Giver** is someone who does not give. The **Reluctant Giver** gives on occasion, likely special events or specific requests, and does so out a sense of obligation. Their giving is not consistent, nor inspired by their gratitude for the grace He has given us. The **Obedient Giver** gives because they think it's the "right thing to do" so they have made a determined decision to do so, possibly motivated by guilt. They follow through consistently, but their heart is not in it. The **Grateful Giver** is motivated by gratitude, as described above.

WHY DOES GOD WANT US TO BECOME A GRATEFUL AND GENEROUS GIVER?

- So He can have full access to our heart, with no distractions
- So we will remember that He alone owns everything
- To reduce financial anxiety in our life
- To prevent or eradicate greed, selfishness, and pride
- So we learn to be content in all circumstances
- So we can experience the blessing of "the shared joy of the master"

Proverbs 11:24 (NIV)
One person gives freely, yet gains even more; another withholds unduly, but comes to poverty.

John 10:10 (NASB)
I came that they may have life, and have it abundantly.

DISCOVERING AND DEMOLISHING STRONGHOLDS

STRONGHOLD: INFERIOR MOTIVATIONS ABOUT GIVING

God's original design as laid out in Scripture regarding the priority for money in the life of a follower of Jesus is crystal clear: "Give First, Lifestyle Last." It is also clear God designed it this way as a blessing *for us*, leading to a more intimate relationship with Him. He wants us to experience the peace and joy that always comes with giving. He intended giving to be motivated out of a heart that is filled with gratitude for the "indescribable" gift of His Son. Every other motivation to give is "*inferior,*" not designed by God but an influence of Mammon. This can be everything from an apathetic view of God's expectations about giving to a conscious decision to disobey His truths.

DIAGNOSTIC STATEMENTS

Consider the following statements, checking each one as it applies to you, to help identify whether "Inferior Motivations" have a negative influence in your life:

- ❏ I don't give to my church because they "always talk about money."
- ❏ I only give when requests are made for special programs that I agree with.
- ❏ I can't afford to give 10% to my church.
- ❏ I don't give money, but I give my time, and that's really the same.
- ❏ I don't think my church needs the money.
- ❏ I would be embarrassed if someone found out how much I give.
- ❏ I don't trust the church leadership to use the money the way I think they should.
- ❏ I am a dutiful giver, but there is no joy in it.
- ❏ I know my giving is nearly zero.
- ❏ If I'm really honest with myself, the reason I give is I feel guilty if I don't give.
- ❏ Giving has nothing to do with my faith.
- ❏ When I give money, I worry that I may need it for something later.
- ❏ I will give more later because right now I'm working to pay off debt or build up my savings.
- ❏ Deep down, part of my reason for giving money is that God will bless me with even more.
- ❏ I am less grateful to God for what I have than I should be.
- ❏ I believe the amount I am able to give is so small it won't matter to the church.

SPIRITUAL TRANSACTION FOR "INFERIOR MOTIVATIONS" USING THE 4RS PRAYER MODEL

1. <u>REPENT</u> – Turn away from "Inferior Motivations" about giving and turn toward God as He created you.

Sample Prayer – Father, I know now that the motivations behind when I give, how I give, and how much I give have been in opposition to Your intentions for me. Please forgive me for my disobedience to You regarding my inferior motivations for giving, for my ingratitude towards what You have provided to me, and for my choices to prioritize my money in ways I want to, rather than in ways You want me to. I acknowledge this as sin and I repent of it.

2. <u>REBUKE</u> – Rebuke Mammon and every other evil spirit influencing this area of your life, including guilt and "inferior motivations" for giving.

Sample Prayer – In Jesus' powerful name, I rebuke Mammon and every evil spirit in my life that has caused me to respond with guilt and all other "inferior motivations" for giving. I resist and refuse to believe the lies about whether I should give, and the lies I have believed about my motivation to give. I break off Mammon and every evil spirit causing me to choose this behavior in my life.

3. <u>REPLACE</u> – Replace every lie or false thought with God's truth.

Sample Prayer – Father, right now I replace every lie and falsehood with Your truth. I claim victory in my life in Your truth that You designed me to be a grateful and generous giver. I claim as truth in my life that I am motivated to give generously purely out of my gratitude for all You have given to me. At all times, I will live with contentment in Your will for my life.

4. <u>RECEIVE</u> – Receive the Lord's promise of forgiveness, His truth, and a fresh infilling of the Holy Spirit.

Sample Prayer – Father, I ask Your Holy Spirit to fill me with a fresh abundance of Your blessings of peace and joy about money, a confidence that Your provision will always be sufficient, and a gratitude for all You have given me. Thank You for the forgiveness You promise me as I come to You in humility. In Jesus' name, Amen.

RELATED SCRIPTURES

Colossians 3:15 (NIV)
Let the peace of Christ rule in your hearts, since as members of one body you were called to peace. And be thankful.

Philippians 3:8 (NLT)
Yes, everything else is worthless when compared with the infinite value of knowing Christ Jesus my Lord. For his sake I have discarded everything else, counting it all as garbage, so that I could gain Christ

2 Corinthians 9:8 (NLT)
And God will generously provide all you need. Then you will always have everything you need and plenty left over to share with others.

PRACTICAL APPLICATION – WALKING IN THE OPPOSITE DIRECTION

- ❏ I will be grateful for each day, and for all God has provided.
- ❏ I will reorder the priorities of my finances to ensure giving comes first.
- ❏ I don't give to my church now, but I will begin giving at least something to get started, until I can get the priorities in alignment with His.
- ❏ I will claim gratitude as my motivation for giving.
- ❏ I will frequently review the four characteristics of an acceptable and pleasing gift to God, and ensure my life and actions reflect that.
- ❏ Each day I will ask God to help me keep an eternal perspective in my life, and focus on the "treasures in Heaven."
- ❏ I will be obedient in all God asks of me in this area of my life.

© John Jonez 2024. All Rights Reserved.

SECTION SIX
What Does a Good Steward Look Like?

Notes: _____

As we covered in Section III, a good steward is faithful to the owner (1 Corinthians 4:2), and trustworthy as a manager (Luke 16:10). Being faithful and trustworthy to God in all He asks of us will bring peace and joy.

Let's look at some ways this peace and joy can be robbed from us, resulting in a level of anxiety.

Anxiety Chart

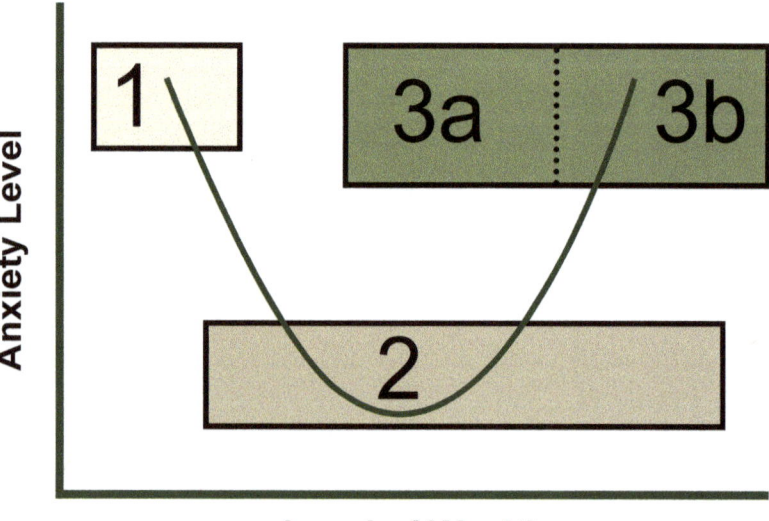

This diagram is a concept chart depicting three different groups of people having various levels of wealth, low to high, and the level of anxiety they experience *given* their level of wealth. People in each of the three groups span a fairly wide range of wealth and also experience either a generally low or generally high level of anxiety. The exact dimensions of each rectangle on the chart are not precise. Each of these groups contains followers of Jesus, as well as those who do not follow Him. Also note: God does not value those who live in poverty, or those who live in great abundance, any higher or lower than anyone else. He specifically cares about what we do with what we have, and whether or not we are faithful with it.

Group 1: Low wealth, high anxiety

This group includes people below the Federal Poverty Level (FPL), as well as a large group called "ALICE," which stands for "<u>A</u>sset <u>L</u>imited <u>I</u>ncome <u>C</u>onstrained <u>E</u>mployed" and comprises people who earn an income just above the poverty level.[19] Combining these two subgroups, they represent 42% of all US households, so it is a very large number of people. The ALICE group alone is 29%. Characteristics of these people include:

- Living paycheck to paycheck, with an income that often does not keep pace with inflation
- Struggling to afford the basic daily needs of life
- Being forced to make unimaginable choices like:
  » Pay the rent or buy food?
  » Pay utility bills or put gas in the car?
  » Pay for medical care or child care?
- Because of these issues, the level of anxiety is usually very high.

Group 3a and 3b: High wealth, high anxiety

This group includes people with levels of wealth well above Group 1, starting just below middle-class all the way up to the very wealthy. The level of anxiety this group experiences is also very high, but obviously for different reasons than those in Group #1.

Group 3a (subset of Group 3): High debt, high anxiety

- Survival is not at risk and basic needs are met.
- May be deeply in debt, buying things before they can afford them
- Striving for a lifestyle that is financially "just out of reach"

© John Jonez 2024. All Rights Reserved.

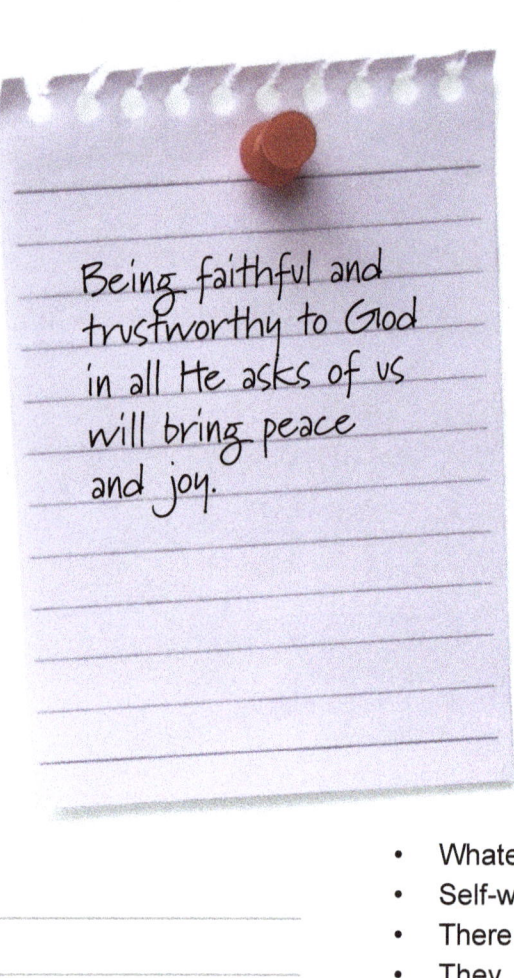

Being faithful and trustworthy to God in all He asks of us will bring peace and joy.

- Savings is insufficient.
- Charitable giving and personal budgeting are usually sporadic or nonexistent.
- Financial health may be getting worse over time, marked by increasing debt.
- Anxiety is usually high relating to:
  » Fear of not having enough money to pay this month's bills due to their over-spending
  » Lack of sufficient savings to cover the costly "unplanned surprises" of life

Group 3b (subset of Group 3): High wealth, high anxiety

- These are people among the upper middle-class and into the top 10%.
- Basic needs are not even thought about.
- Most "wants" can be met.
- Costly surprises of life are easily taken care of.
- They are driven by and for success.
- Whatever their level of wealth, it is not enough.
- Self-worth and their identity may be defined by their wealth.
- There is no finish line; more is always better.
- They seek fulfillment and often find emptiness—"Is that all there is?"
- Anxiety is often very high due to:
  » The drive for an appearance of high wealth
  » Comparison to others within this group

Group 2: Low to high wealth, low anxiety

In this group, the level of wealth is very wide, as low as some in Group 1, and as high as many in Group 3. How can they have low anxiety? These people's characteristics can include:

- They are grateful for and content with what they have, whatever their circumstances.
- At higher levels of wealth, they view it as more than they need, and seek to find ways to help others.
- Raising the standard of living above their level of contentment is not important.
- They manage their money well and have plenty of "margin" in their finances.
- They are often described as generous.
- They use money to serve people, rather than using people to serve money.
- They value relationships more than money and things.

- If they follow Jesus, they are secure in their faith and know their true treasure is a "priceless inheritance" (1 Peter 1:4), kept in Heaven for them.
- Their level of anxiety is low, just how God designed it.

FOR REVIEW: MONEY PRIORITIZATION AS GOD DESIGNED IT (WE ARE TO BE FAITHFUL)

1. Giving – Our highest priority, because we are grateful
2. Saving – There is wisdom in saving.
3. Debt – It is dangerous, and comes with a cautionary warning.
4. Lifestyle Spending – Last Priority. Contentment is a virtue.

God's request for His people to be faithful, and His reward for those who are faithful, is best seen in the Parable of the Talents in Matthew 25:14–30. A talent is an amount of money, but the parable is about everything we have, and every minute we are alive.

THE PARABLE OF THE TALENTS – ILLUSTRATING THE KINGDOM OF HEAVEN

Summary of Matthew 25:14-30 (NIV)
Before a Master left on a journey, he entrusted some of his money to three of his servants. To one servant he gave five talents, to another two talents, and to another one talent, in proportion to their abilities. Upon his return, he called the servants together to obtain an account of what they did with his money. Both the five-talent servant and the two-talent servant had invested the money and doubled the amount for the

> Jesus expects faithfulness from His followers, and the reward is great!

master. However, the one-talent servant, out of fear and spite for his master, buried the money and returned the one talent to him.

To the five-talent servant, the Master said:

Matthew 25:21 (AMP)

"Well done, good and faithful servant. You have been faithful and trustworthy over a little, I will put you in charge of many things; share in the joy of your master."

To the two-talent servant, the Master said:

Matthew 25:23 (AMP)

"Well done, good and faithful servant. You have been faithful and trustworthy over a little, I will put you in charge of many things; share in the joy of your master."

The Master called the one-talent servant "wicked, lazy, and worthless." The Master then took the one talent from him and gave it to the servant who had 10 talents.

The meaning of this story is that Jesus expects faithfulness from His followers, and the reward is great: "Come and share in the joy of your Master." What could be better than experiencing the joy of our King? Those who live today with a future perspective of His eternal Kingdom, knowing one day when He returns, we will give an account of all we have done, will receive great rewards.

© John Jonez 2024. All Rights Reserved.

We have spent the majority of this study developing a deep understanding of giving which, according to God's design, is the first and highest priority we have for His money. We will now explore Saving, Debt, and Lifestyle Spending.

SAVING – THERE IS WISDOM IN SAVING (DELAYED SPENDING)

> Those who live today with a future perspective of His eternal Kingdom, knowing one day when He returns, we will give an account of all we have done, will receive great rewards.

Proverbs 21:20 (NIV)
The wise store up choice food and olive oil, but fools gulp theirs down.

Proverbs 21:20 (NLT)
The wise have wealth and luxury, but fools spend whatever they get.

WISE SAVING:
1. For unknown future needs
    a. Emergency Fund – For the unexpected, absolutely necessary, and immediate things.
    b. Six to Nine Months of Living Expenses – For an unexpected job loss or other income interruption.
2. For known future needs
    a. To buy the next car
    b. To buy a home
    c. To pay for children's college
    d. Retirement
3. To be able to respond to God's unforeseen calling
    a. He may ask you to give to someone in need.
    b. He may ask you to go on a mission trip.
    c. The Good Samaritan (Luke 10:30–37) was a good steward.
4. To demonstrate discipline, delayed gratification, and contentment

FOOLISH SAVING:
1. No savings, minimal savings, and inconsistently adding to savings
2. Hoarding

Luke 12:16–21 (NLT) – Hoarding
"A rich man had a fertile farm that produced fine crops. He said to himself, 'What should I do? I don't have room for all my crops.' Then he said, 'I know! I'll tear down my barns and build bigger ones. Then I'll have room enough to store all my wheat and other goods. And I'll sit back and say to myself, "My friend, you have enough stored away for years to come. Now take it easy! Eat, drink, and be merry!"' "But God

said to him, 'You fool! You will die this very night. Then who will get everything you worked for?' "Yes, a person is a fool to store up earthly wealth but not have a rich relationship with God."

"But godliness with contentment is great gain."
1 Timothy 6:6

DEBT—IT IS DANGEROUS AND COMES WITH A CAUTIONARY WARNING

Proverbs 22:7 (NIV)
The rich rule over the poor, and the borrower is slave to the lender.

Carrying excessive debt can easily rob us of our freedom, limit our choices both now and in the future, and substantially raise our level of anxiety. While debt is not a sin, Jesus wants us to live in freedom—free from the stresses caused by mismanagement of *His* money.

While we are well aware of the difficulties many people face with the issue of debt, the specific practical steps to deal with it are beyond the scope of this study. That said, there is hope and help if needed, and encourage you to see Step #5 in the last section of this book.

LIFESTYLE SPENDING—LAST PRIORITY (CONTENTMENT IS A VIRTUE)

Consider these four kinds of spenders:

1. Spontaneous Spender – Impulsive. Sees it, wants it now. No plan. In debt.
2. Fearful Spender – Spends in fear and uncertainty. No plan. "Cheapskate." May be hoarding money.
3. Scarcity Spender – "I'm too poor." Can't spend, a poverty spirit. Intentionally hoarding money.
4. Careful Spender –
   - Has a plan, knows what they can afford, and spends in freedom
   - Enjoys life along the way
   - Ready for emergencies
   - Content in all circumstances
   - Priorities are in the correct order

Obviously, by the descriptions of these four types of spenders, the advantages of being a careful spender are obvious and therefore it is the best type to emulate. However, for a follower of Jesus, even this careful spender may not be carrying out God's expectation to be "faithful to the owner and trustworthy as a manager." That high calling depends on *how* we spend. Are we just a careful spender, or a Kingdom investor? As Matthew 6:19–21 tells us, we are to *store up treasures in Heaven*, and giving money away or spending it for Kingdom purposes are both examples of this.

SPENDERS VERSUS KINGDOM INVESTORS

With all God has entrusted to us, we can choose to use it in one of three ways:

1. Waste it – No one chooses this; they discover it in retrospect, when it is too late.
2. Spend it – Excessively focused on ourselves
3. Invest it – In God's Kingdom
    - For the good of others
    - For our own growth as disciples
    - For the glory of God

Matthew 6:19–21 (NIV)

Do not store up for yourselves treasures on earth, where moth and rust destroy, and where thieves break in and steal. But store up for yourselves treasures in heaven, where moth and rust do not destroy, and where thieves do not break in and steal. For where your treasure is, there your heart will be also.

Look at this last sentence in these verses "For where your treasure is, there your heart will be also." It is clear—whatever we value most is our treasure. If we value our bank account, our career, our possessions, our lofty corporate title, or anything else above our relationship with Jesus, then these other things are our treasure, and our heart will be with them. It is impossible to value these things above Him, yet claim our heart follows Him. Our heart follows our treasure, not the other way around.

DECLARATIONS TO GOD IN PRAYER:

Father, we come with a renewed sense of your teachings about money and, before You, we make the following declarations:

- We understand Mammon's singular evil mission is to entice us away from following You, to deceive us about Your truths replacing them with his lies, and prevent us from living in those truths in our daily life.
- In humility, we submit our hearts and finances to You.
- We acknowledge that our money is actually Your money.
- We will not allow money to be a distraction in our walk with You.

- We will cling to the Your truths in Scripture as outlined throughout this study.
- We declare that You alone are whom we worship and follow, unencumbered by the distractions, influences, and fears around money.
- We ask the Holy Spirit to guide us to manage well, and to live generous lives.
- In the precious name of your Son, Jesus, Amen.

PAUL'S CHARGE TO TIMOTHY—THE GOLD STANDARD OF THE GOOD STEWARD

1 Timothy 6:17–19 (NIV)
Command those who are rich in this present world not to be arrogant nor to put their hope in wealth, which is so uncertain, but to put their hope in God, who richly provides us with everything for our enjoyment. Command them to do good, to be rich in good deeds, and to be generous and willing to share. In this way they will lay up treasure for themselves as a firm foundation for the coming age, so that they may take hold of the life that is truly life.

WHAT REWARDS AWAIT THE GOOD STEWARD?

- God gives us everything for our enjoyment (1 Timothy 6:17). If we manage His money according to His design, we will enjoy it all.
- We will hear, "Well done, good and faithful servant," and we will share in the joy of our Master. (Matthew 25: 21,23)
- We have a priceless and eternal inheritance kept in Heaven for us (1 Peter 1:4).

1 Corinthians 2:9 (NLT)
"No eye has seen, no ear has heard, and no mind has imagined what God has prepared for those who love him."

We have a priceless and eternal inheritance kept in Heaven for us (1 Peter 1:4).

SECTION SEVEN
Getting Practical: Where Do We Begin?

Through this study, God may be leading you to make some changes in your life, possibly a reordering of priorities. God is a perfect and loving Father who wants the very best for us, and we should be grateful to Him for sending Jesus to restore our personal relationship with the Father, and to bring every area of our life—including finances—into alignment with His Word and will.

Where does a person begin?

1. PRAY.

Pray, then pray some more. Keep praying. Don't stop. This step is critical.

1 Thessalonians 5:16–18 (NIV)
Rejoice always, pray continually, give thanks in all circumstances; for this is God's will for you in Christ Jesus.

2. CREATE A MONTHLY SPENDING PLAN.

For many people, budgeting is not very exciting. In fact, some people absolutely hate it! "I don't want to be controlled by a budget!!" Instead of calling it a budget, let's call it a Spending Plan – after all, *spending* money sounds better than *budgeting* money.

If you have not routinely created a monthly spending plan and tracked actual expenses against it for comparison, now is the time to start. There's an old saying in the business world: "If you don't *measure* it, you can't *manage* it." It is true!

The purpose of such a plan is not to tell you what you can't do, but to tell what you can do. This allows you to spend in freedom, knowing that "the numbers all work out," short term and long term, and your level of anxiety will begin to come down.

Many people have never set up a spending plan. If you really have no idea how to determine what you might spend in the various expense categories, then skip the *plan* part and start by simply tracking your *actual* income and expenses for a month or two. Separate expenses into the categories shown below. This will give you some information to use and create a spending *plan* for future months. Whatever you do, do not go back in time and attempt to recreate an accounting of your expenses from prior months. It sounds like a good idea, but it will be the most frustrating exercise you have ever done, and it is unlikely to give you any useful information.

The spending plan must include all outgoing expenditures, including charitable giving. Even if you can only give a small amount to begin with, just remember, it is the heart behind the gift that matters. God will honor your gifts, even small ones, as you begin to develop the habit of giving. A more robust plan for giving should be developed as your priorities begin to match His original design.

In the Appendix of this manual, you will find a sample spending plan worksheet. Feel free to use this one and modify it. Or, find one online you like or start with a blank sheet of paper to create your own. After you do this for a couple of months, you may choose to use an app-based budgeting tool; "EveryDollar" is a popular one. If you have too many categories, the exercise gets more difficult. But if you have too few categories, the "miscellaneous" category will become too big to provide insight for making tradeoffs between categories as needed.

© John Jonez 2024. All Rights Reserved.

3. COMPARE YOUR SPENDING BY CATEGORY TO EXPERT RECOMMENDATIONS.

Once you have some actual data about your spending in various categories, it is really helpful to compare that to recommendations made by financial experts. It will highlight areas requiring attention. For example, if you live in a geography with a higher average cost for housing, you will need to offset it with a lower amount in another category. Here is one such set of guidelines, and you'll find detailed explanations of these categories in Appendix C:[20]

1. Charitable Giving (10%+)
2. Housing (25%–35%)
3. Transportation (10%–15%)
4. Food and Dining Out (10%–20%)
5. Utilities (5%–10%)
6. Insurance (10%–25%)
7. Medical and Healthcare (5%–10%)
8. Debt Payments (0%)
9. Savings and Investments (10%–20%)
10. Personal Spending (5%–10%)
11. Recreation and Entertainment (5%–10%)
12. Miscellaneous (5%)

4. REVIEW THE PERSONAL MONEY MANAGEMENT ASSESSMENT IN THE APPENDIX.

If married, both spouses should fill out this assessment individually and then compare answers with one another. Some of the answers will not match at all. For example, one spouse might prefer having a root canal rather than deal with a spending plan, but the other spouse actually enjoys it (the spending plan, not the root canal). This assessment will help you determine the areas of your financial life requiring additional focus. Why would God want you to manage your finances well? Because He owns everything, and wants us to be faithful managers.

5. REVIEW ALL CONSUMER DEBT, AND GET IT PAID OFF.

If you carry any significant consumer debt, we highly recommend signing up for Dave Ramsey's Financial Peace University in your local area. (www.RamseySolutions.com) Follow his guidance through the "Baby Steps."

> *Once you have some actual data about your spending in various categories, it is helpful to compare that to recommendations made by financial experts.*

6. BEGIN SAVING FOR RETIREMENT AS SOON AS POSSIBLE.

One of the hardest financial questions to answer is, "How much do I need to save every month, starting now, to have enough money to retire at my desired retirement age with the lifestyle I want?" Going through Financial Peace University will give you some direction to get started. But meeting with a Certified Financial Planner, if for no other reason than to get an answer to this question, is a very wise move. Too many people wait until it is really too late to focus on this, and retire with insufficient funds to support themselves with a satisfactory lifestyle. Social Security will not be sufficient by itself.

7. DEVELOP A PLAN FOR GENEROUS GIVING.

This step can be a journey for most people—how much should I give, and to what causes? These are big questions with very different answers from person to person, and there is not necessarily one right answer, but some guidance and suggestions may help. First, be sure you have an "operational" spending plan—updated monthly—a plan with actual spending tracked against it.

If you are barely getting by financially month to month, then focusing on the realignment of your spending and income must come first. But early in this process, begin giving *something*—just start. Even a small amount will start the process of becoming consistent in this area.

As your financial life gets healthier, it will seem natural for your level of giving to increase. The good news is YOU determine the amount (2 Corinthians 9:7), an amount "you have decided in your heart." Remember, the *amount* has to matter to you; then it will matter to God.

Regarding *where* to give, we highly recommend giving to your local church first and foremost. The local church is critically important to the Kingdom of God on this earth. As believers, we should be receiving food for spiritual growth from our church. We need to belong to a church, serve actively in it, and give generously.

1 Timothy 5:18 (NIV)
For Scripture says, "Do not muzzle an ox while it is treading out the grain," and "The worker deserves his wages."

© John Jonez 2024. All Rights Reserved.

Your church staff deserves to be paid well, just as the ox working in the field deserves to eat. From the giver's viewpoint, this type of "no strings attached" giving is the purest act of surrender to God's calling.

When deciding where to give *in addition* to your church, it is helpful to consider those "Causes and Passions" in Appendix F that tug at your heart.[21] God put those passions inside of you for a reason, both to help you decide where to *serve* and where to *give*.

A TESTIMONY: BOB AND JULIE'S "GIVING JOURNEY"

"As our giving increased over time, we began receiving a greater number of requests to give to various causes. We felt an obligation to give something to all of them, and if we ever denied a request to give, we felt guilty about it. We knew that was not what God wanted for us. We began to pray about a giving strategy and asked God what causes He wanted us to focus on.

He placed on our hearts the conviction that His Church was the highest priority for giving. His Church is His structure on Earth for His Kingdom, and it is the hope of the world. We see our giving as one way of demonstrating surrender to God for all He has given us. Therefore, we prioritize giving 10 percent to our local church.

After that, He placed on our hearts the idea of "Second Chances." Jesus gave us all the ultimate second chance at eternity through the forgiveness of our sins, and a restored relationship with God the Father. This category for our giving includes opportunities where people can be offered a second chance to find hope in Jesus, and meet their physical, emotional, and spiritual needs. This is a broad category requiring discernment, so we also rely heavily on those areas that "tug" on our hearts.

The third category includes places where the three of us serve together—husband, wife, and Jesus.

Although He placed this on our hearts, we still pray God will show us specific areas He would have us give. One benefit is we now have the freedom to say "no" to requests not fitting these guidelines, without guilt, and our joy of giving is at an all-time high."

We highly recommend the development of your own "Giving Strategy." If you work on it proactively, it will bring married couples closer together, bring you closer to God and His calling on your life, and bring you more joy in the act of giving than you can imagine.

DISCOVERING AND DEMOLISHING STRONGHOLDS

STRONGHOLD: PASSIVITY

Passivity (Definition) – "Failure to take action when action is necessary"

Through this study, you may have discovered the need to make some changes in how you view and manage money. In this section, after continuing to uphold your efforts in prayer, the most basic, practical, and important action needed is the creation of a spending plan.

"Managing" anything—in particular, managing money—and especially when managing it for the benefit of someone else (God's money, entrusted to us), requires action. As we said before, "If you don't *measure* it, you can't *manage* it." Without an active spending plan, it is impossible to manage money. Refusing to "manage" is an abdication of our responsibility in the role God has placed us. Failure to do so is called "passivity."

DIAGNOSTIC STATEMENTS

Consider the following statements, checking each one as it applies to you, to help identify where passivity has an influence in your life:

- ❏ I often avoid things I don't like to do.
- ❏ I'm more inclined to do things I like to do than what I ought to do.
- ❏ Passivity is "just how I'm wired"; that's how God made me.
- ❏ I am not motivated to develop a more intimate relationship with God.
- ❏ I tend to avoid things outside my comfort zone, even if I know they are important.
- ❏ I am my own person, and will do things my own way.
- ❏ Mom and Dad called me the "shy one," and they are right.
- ❏ I usually wait for others to take the lead.
- ❏ I prefer to sit back and watch others, but not engage myself.
- ❏ If I'm honest with myself, procrastination is a regular pattern in my life.
- ❏ Because I'm a good person, I don't see sin in my life very often.
- ❏ I can look back and see problems created that I could have avoided.
- ❏ God likes me just the way I am; I don't see a need to change.

SPIRITUAL TRANSACTION FOR "PASSIVITY" USING THE 4RS PRAYER MODEL

1. <u>REPENT</u> – Turn away from passivity and toward things God would have me do.

Sample Prayer – Father, I ask for Your forgiveness for the sin of living in passivity, and for the patterns of passivity in my life. Passivity is not from You! I repent of every way I have chosen passivity to be a part of my personality and behavior, and for how it has affected the people around me. I commit to breaking these patterns in my life.

2. <u>REBUKE</u> – Rebuke Mammon and every other evil spirit influencing this area of your life.

Sample Prayer – Right now I rebuke Mammon and every evil spirit in my life that has caused me to choose to live in passivity. By the authority of Jesus, I come against you right now and command you to flee from any influence in my life. Father, You didn't design me to be passive, especially about my relationship with You and all that You would have me do.

3. <u>REPLACE</u> – Replace every lie or false thought with God's truth.

Sample Prayer – Father, I declare by Your grace that I will live my life in obedience to You, immediately, completely, and joyfully. I will proactively seek help from others as needed in the areas of managing Your money on Your behalf, as You would have me do.

4. <u>RECEIVE</u> – Receive the Lord's promise of forgiveness, His truth, and a fresh infilling of the Holy Spirit.

Sample Prayer – Father, I ask and receive the filling of Your Holy Spirit into my life right now so I can live a life of faith and obedience in Your truth. Thank You for forgiving me and cleansing me. I humbly receive Your forgiveness. In Jesus' Name, Amen

RELATED SCRIPTURES

Philippians 4:13 (NIV)
I can do all this through him who gives me strength.

1 Timothy 6:11b (NLT)
Pursue righteousness and a godly life, along with faith, love, perseverance, and gentleness.

2 Timothy 1:7 (NLT)
For God has not given us a spirit of fear and timidity, but of power, love, and self-discipline.

Proverbs 12:24 (NIV)
Diligent hands will rule, but laziness ends in forced labor.

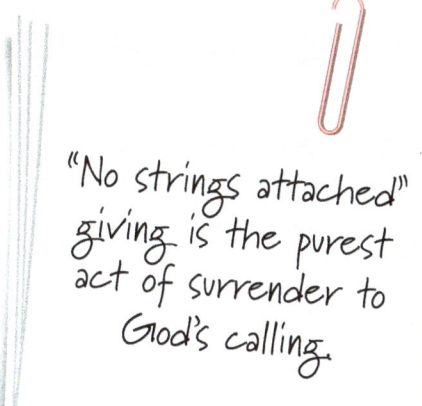

"No strings attached" giving is the purest act of surrender to God's calling.

PRACTICAL APPLICATION – WALKING IN THE OPPOSITE DIRECTION

- ❏ I will be proactive in managing my finances.
- ❏ I will work together with my spouse (if married) on all financial issues.
- ❏ I will get professional help in areas I'm uncertain about related to my finances.
- ❏ I will create a spending plan and track actual income and expenses against that plan each month.
- ❏ I will develop my spending plan to include the elimination of all consumer debt.
- ❏ I will establish a giving plan fully funded within my spending plan.
- ❏ I will establish a saving plan fully funded within my spending plan.
- ❏ I will utilize the "Spending Decision Tool" in the Appendix to this book.
- ❏ Large financial decisions will be made in collaboration with my spouse.

Group Discussion Questions

Notes:

The author believes the learning process for many people involves contemplation and sharing real-life experiences with other participants, resulting in self-discovery of useful application in their own life. That said, the discussion must focus on clarifying what they learned, sharing examples from their own life relating to the material presented, and considering how the truths presented may be applied. Discussion should not focus on speculation about the truths in Scripture as they are presented.

DISCUSSION FOR SECTION I

This section is exclusively teaching about Biblical truths and tools to use in application of the information presented in the remainder of the sections. If this material is being presented in a workshop, small group, or discipleship scenario, the leader should ask participants if they have questions about the content presented to determine if clarification is needed. This time can be used getting to know one another, inviting discussion on what each participant hopes to learn in the course, and praying for one another.

DISCUSSION QUESTIONS FOR SECTION II

1. Whether or not you had ever heard about or known what or who Mammon is, can you share any areas of your life where you can now realize this spirit has influenced you?

2. Comparing the two masters, God and Mammon, which of their differences is most striking to you and why?

3. Why did Jesus choose money or Mammon as the only "other master" He ever compared to God?

4. Is the lack of generosity only a "rich-person" issue?

DISCUSSION QUESTIONS FOR SECTION III

1. How will you live as a *manager* rather than an *owner* when our economic system is often centered around private property ownership?

2. How will you live as *manager* rather than an *owner* when the American culture is often driven by a relentless pursuit of worldly success?

3. How has the culture influenced your attitudes or behaviors related to money?

4. How do you prioritize money, as it relates to the culture's version of "Lifestyle First," and "Giving Last"?

DISCUSSION QUESTIONS FOR SECTION IV

1. How does the phrase "giving is an act of worship"—with "worship" defined as "to honor, obey, and emulate Jesus by how we live"—manifest itself in your life?

2. How do you see it possible to live prioritizing money as God designed it—giving first, lifestyle funding last?

3. The Bible defines faith in Hebrews 11:1 as "Faith is being *sure* of what we hope for, and *certain* of what we cannot see." How does your life demonstrate you are *sure* and *certain*? How does your relationship with money reflect that?

4. How do your faith and giving relate to your perspective of Mammon?

GROUP DISCUSSION QUESTIONS FOR SECTION V

1. Do you think "being generous leads to a grateful heart" and "a grateful heart leads to being generous" can both be true at the same time? How does your gratitude influence your giving?

2. How do you view generosity as a pathway to a more intimate relationship with God?

3. Share with the group one way you practice gratitude.

4. Can we have a grateful heart if we never experience God's grace as described in 2 Corinthians chapters 8 and 9?

© John Jonez 2024. All Rights Reserved.

GROUP DISCUSSION QUESTIONS FOR SECTION VI

1. Share how the "Four Kinds of Spenders" list resonates with you. What has been your journey regarding spending?

2. How does your life represent being a Kingdom Investor? Is being a Kingdom Investor all about money? If not, what else is involved?

3. First Timothy 6:17 (NIV) says, "God gives us everything for our enjoyment." How can you balance spending money on things "for your enjoyment" versus "investing in the Kingdom"? Are these two ideas mutually exclusive?

4. What are the areas in your life where Mammon has stolen your freedom in Christ?

DISCUSSION QUESTIONS FOR SECTION VII

1. Please share with the group if you use a budget, and if so, how you prepare it and use it to track expenses.

2. When considering large purchases, how do you and your spouse work together to make the decision to proceed or not proceed with the purchase?

3. If you realized that the stronghold of passivity has played a role in your finances, what commitment will you make today to manage God's money more proactively?

4. How does the testimony of Bob and Julie's giving journey motivate you in your own giving?

© John Jonez 2024. All Rights Reserved.

Appendix

Personal Money Management Assessment

Protection	1	2	3	4	5
Health Insurance	None		Catastrophic only		Sufficient coverage
Life Insurance	None		Burial insurance only		Sufficient coverage
Homeowner's or Renters Insurance	None				Sufficient coverage
Auto Insurance	None		Collision Only		Full Coverage
Long Term Disability Insurance	None				Sufficient coverage
Umbrella Policy	None				Sufficient coverage
Estate Plan Documents. These include: 1. Directive to Physicans & Family 2. Statement Regarding Anatomical Gifts 3. Medical Power of Attorney 4. Declaration of Guardian for Minor Children 5. Declaration of Guardian for Myself 6. Appointment of Agent to Control Disposition of Remains 7. Statutory Durable Power of Attorney 8. Last Will and Testament.	None		Last Will and Testament Only		Documents are in place and up-to-date for both my spouse and I

Budgeting	1	2	3	4	5
My personal view on budgeting	Hate it		Do it. Don't like it.		Budgets create freedom
We have a written budget	None		Occasionally Budget		Monthly with Actual spending tracking
My spouse and I collaborate on the development of our budget	None		One of us does it		Work Together
Our budget includes ongoing and consistent charitable giving	None		Not included in budget		Included and routinely give
Our budget includes future known expenses, and we set that money aside each month	None		Excluded from Budget		Budget Includes future expenses.

Spending	1	2	3	4	5
We spend less than we earn	We don't know		Paycheck to paycheck		Spend < 80% of take home pay
Spending includes consistent charitable giving	There is no money left over to give		We give when we can		Consistently give 10% or more
We track actual expenses against our budget	No		Sometimes		Monthly
Total housing is less than 30% of take-home pay	We don't know		Greater than 30%		30% or less
My spouse and I make large spending decisions together, even if they are included in the budget	Never		Sometimes		Always
Savings	**1**	**2**	**3**	**4**	**5**
We have an emergency fund set aside	Could not pay cash for a $400 surprise		$2500 or more set aside		3-6 months of living expenses
We save monthly for future known expenses	No		Occasionally		Always
We save for retirement monthly	No		Yes, but we are behind		On track, and contribute monthly
We worked with a financial advisor to create a plan to know our monthly saving goal in order to retire with dignity.	No		That's a good idea		Done and saving accordingly
We demonstrate to our children the value of saving money.	No		Sometimes		Actively
Debt	**1**	**2**	**3**	**4**	**5**
How much debt other than my mortgage?	Drowning in Debt		Some debt and actively paying it off	No debt. Just our mortgage	No debt, mortgage paid off
How do I feel about the amount of debt I have now?	Highly concerned, where do I start?		Concerned, but actively paying it off		No debt other than my mortgage
Other than our mortgage, we pay cash for everything.	Routinely use consumer debt		Occasionally use debt to buy things		Yes
Use of credit cards	Routinely use them, balance is growing		Occasionally use, balance fluctuates	Consistently use & pay off monthly	Do not use them
Use of other consumer debt, home equity loans, car loans.	We use this kind of debt routinely		Have some, working to pay off		No debt outside of our mortgage

© John Jonez 2024. All Rights Reserved.

Spending Plan Worksheet

Income (excluding investment income)	Actual	Plan	Difference
Paycheck #1			
Paycheck #2			
Other Income			
Total:			

Expenses

Charitable Giving (10%+ Goal)	Actual	Plan	Difference
Charity #1			
Charity #2			
Charity #3			
Subtotal:			

Housing (25% - 35%)	Actual	Plan	Difference
Rent or Mortgage			
Property Taxes			
Homeowner Association Dues			
Maintenance			
Home Furnishings & Décor			
Security			
Other			
Subtotal:			

Transportation (10% - 15%)	Actual	Plan	Difference
Car Payments			
Registration Fees			
Gas			
Maintenance			
Parking & Tolls			
Public Transportation			
Subtotal:			

Food (10% - 20%)	Actual	Plan	Difference
Groceries & Paper Products			
Dining Out			
Subtotal:			

Utilities (5% - 10%)	Actual	Plan	Difference
Gas			
Electricity			
Water & Sewer			
Phone			
Internet			
TV & Streaming			
Subtotal:			

Insurance (10% - 25%)	Actual	Plan	Difference
Health Insurance (Medical, Dental, Vision)			

Homeowner's or Renter's Insurance			
Home Warranty Insurance			
Auto Insurance			
Life Insurance			
Disability Insurance			
Subtotal:			
Medical and Healthcare (5% - 10%)	**Actual**	**Plan**	**Difference**
Out of Pocket Copays and Deductibles			
Dental Care			
Vision Care			
Perscriptions & OTC Medications			
Other Medical			
Subtotal:			
Debt Payments (0% Goal)	**Actual**	**Plan**	**Difference**
Credit Card #1			
Credit Card #2			
Credit Card #3			
Student Loans			
Other debt			
Other debt			
Subtotal:			
Savings & Investments (10% - 20%)	**Actual**	**Plan**	**Difference**
Emergency Fund			
6-9 Months Living Expenses			
Retirement			
Car Replacement Fund			
Children's College Fund			
Vacation Fund			
Subtotal:			
Personal Spending (10% - 15%)	**Actual**	**Plan**	**Difference**
Child Care			
Gym Memberships			
Clothing			
Gifts			
Other			
Subtotal:			
Recreation and Entertainment (5% - 10%)	**Actual**	**Plan**	**Difference**
Concert Tickets & Sporting Events			
Hobbies			
Vacations			
Subtotal:			
Miscellaneous (5% Max)			
Subtotal:			
Grand Total			

SPENDING PLAN CATEGORY DESCRIPTIONS

1. CHARITABLE GIVING (10%+)

2. HOUSING (25%–35%): This is often the largest category. It includes your rent or mortgage, property taxes, Homeowner Association dues, maintenance costs, home furnishings and décor, security, etc.

3. TRANSPORTATION (10%–15%): Includes car payments, registration fees, gas, maintenance, parking, tolls, and public transportation

4. FOOD AND DINING OUT (10%–20%): Includes groceries and other grocery store items like paper products, etc. Because of the highly discretionary nature of dining out, it may be a category of its own. It is an area where most people are surprised when they look at the high total amount spent for a month.

5. UTILITIES (5%–10%): Includes natural gas, electricity, water, sewer, phone, internet, TV and streaming charges

6. INSURANCE (10%–25%): Includes health insurance, homeowners' or renters' insurance, home warranty plans, auto insurance, life insurance, and disability insurance. It is recommended to include all insurance in this category rather than putting auto insurance in the transportation category, and Homeowner's insurance in the housing category. The total cost of all insurance is a big number, and looking at it as a total category is helpful.

7. MEDICAL AND HEALTHCARE (5%–10%): Includes out-of-pocket copays and deductibles for doctor and hospital visits, dental and vision care, prescriptions and over-the-counter medications, and medical devices and supplies. The amount in this category will vary widely person to person, depending on needs.

8. DEBT PAYMENTS (0%): This category will vary widely depending on individual circumstances. We include an eventual target of zero debt other than a mortgage.

9. SAVINGS AND INVESTMENTS (10%– 20%): This includes saving for an emergency fund if you do not have one established, ultimately funded at six to nine months of living expenses. Other savings includes funds for infrequent, known expenses like annual insurance payments, very infrequent expenses like the next car, children's college, and ultimately your own retirement.

10. PERSONAL SPENDING (5%–10%): Includes things like gym memberships, clothing, and gifts

11. RECREATION AND ENTERTAINMENT (5%–10%): Concert tickets, sporting events, vacations, and hobbies

12. MISCELLANEOUS (5%): This category is for things that don't fit other categories. If it is more than 5%, then a separate category needs to be made.

SPENDING DECISION TOOL

Luke 14:28 (NLT)
But don't begin until you count the cost. For who would begin construction of a building without first calculating the cost to see if there is enough money to finish it?

This is a simple diagnostic tool to help you make decisions regarding whether to purchase something. It is most relevant when considering "significant" purchases, whatever that might mean in your situation. If this decision relates to a construction or landscaping project of some kind, count on your estimate being low by at least 50%. This tool may not provide a black-and-white answer to the "should I buy it" question, but will likely steer you towards the correct decision. Spouses should discuss significant purchase decisions between them, even if the purchase only benefits one spouse. It's *our* money, not *my* money.

SPENDING DIAGNOSIS: SHOULD I BUY IT?

- ❏ Does my spouse agree with this purchase?
- ❏ Is this item consistent with Scripture and God's character?

IF THE ANSWER IS "NO" TO THESE QUESTIONS, THEN DON'T BUY IT.

- ❏ Is it included in my spending plan or can I make trade-offs within my spending plan to stay on target?
- ❏ Is it an emergency? (Unexpected, Absolutely Necessary, Immediate)

IF THE ANSWER IS "NO" TO THESE QUESTIONS, THEN DON'T BUY IT.

- ❏ Is it a "need" or a "want"? (Be honest.)
- ❏ Does this purchase put at risk the basic necessities for me or my family?
- ❏ Does this purchase put at risk my charitable giving this month?
- ❏ Do I have my emergency fund in place and funded at a minimum of $2500?
- ❏ Do I have at least six months of living expenses set aside?
- ❏ Do I have the cash available now to make this purchase?
- ❏ Have I been thinking about this purchase for a while or is it impulsive?
- ❏ If I wait to buy this item, is it still available later at the same price?
- ❏ Is there a less expensive way to acquire the same item?
- ❏ Is there a less expensive item that would fulfill the same purpose?
- ❏ If no one ever saw me with this item, would I still buy it? In other words, what is my motivation for making this purpose?
- ❏ Does my "gut" (instinct) tell me something about this?

If, after honestly answering these questions, it's unclear whether to make the purchase, then wait until the answer becomes clearer.

BOOK REVIEW: *THE GOLDEN GHETTO, THE PSYCHOLOGY OF AFFLUENCE*

Author: Jessie O'Neill[22]

"The Golden Ghetto" is inhabited by millions of Americans who embrace and endlessly pursue the fantasy that more is better.

About Jessie O'Neill:
- She is the granddaughter of Charles E. Wilson, CEO of General Motors who became Secretary of Defense in 1953 under President Eisenhower. She grew up in an elite family having substantial wealth.
- At age 40, she became a psychotherapist with a professional practice focused exclusively on treating the problems of those who have amassed great wealth or inherited great wealth— both the wealthy and the children of the wealthy.
- Jessie O'Neill popularized the term "affluenza," defined as "the psychological dysfunctions of affluence."
- After years in her practice, she concluded that, at higher levels of wealth:
  » The dysfunction of wealth is generational; hers came from her grandfather.
  » Wealth creates a false sense of entitlement.
  » Inherited wealth often damages self-esteem, self-worth, and confidence.
  » In a wealthy family, because everything is immediate, it results in an inability to handle delayed gratification, control impulse, and effectively manage disappointment and frustration.

About children, according to O'Neill:
- Both rich and poor children suffer from the emotional effects of parents who are frequently absent.
- The lonely child will likely become an adult who struggles to find enough love to fill the emotional void. In rich families, children usually realize the parent's absence was not due to economic necessity, but by their choice of priorities.
- Children need to be affirmed for who they are, not for the "important family" they belong to, nor for their family's wealth.

Jessie's conclusion:
"When we learn to value ourselves simply for who we are, to love our children simply because they are our children, and radically shift our priorities and focus our energies and resources on helping those less fortunate than we are, we will be on our way to create a new American Dream."

The "Affluenza" Defense:[23]
On June 15, 2013, at the age of 16, while driving 70 mph in a 40-mph zone in Burleson, Texas, Ethan Anthony Couch killed four people and injured nine others, one of which was completely paralyzed. He also tested at three times the legal limit for alcohol, and tested positive for both marijuana and Valium. A psychologist at his manslaughter trial blamed his irresponsibility on family wealth, dubbing it "Affluenza." He purportedly did not understand "right and wrong," or "boundaries," because he'd never had any. He was sentenced to two years in prison.

GIVING CAUSES TO CONSIDER

Addiction	Food Supply	Museums
Adoption & Foster Care	Giving and Generosity	Orphan Care
Animal Protection & Welfare	History	Pastoral Care
Apologetics	Homelessness	Police & Fire Department
Arts & Humanities	Housing	Prayer
Bible Translation	Human Rights	Prison Ministry
Children's & Youth Ministry	Human Trafficking	Public Policy
Christian Persecution	Humanitarian Aid & Dev.	Retreat Centers & Camps
Church	Jobs & Workplace	Refugee Support
Church Planting	Leadership Development	Right to Life
Civil Rights	Legal Services	Single Parents & Widows
Colleges & Universities	Marketplace Ministry	Slavery
Community Development	Marriage	Social Justice
Developmental Disabilities	Media & Publishing	Spiritual Development
Disaster Relief	Medical Care	Sports & Recreation
Domestic Violence	Medical Research	Student Ministry
Education	Men's Ministry	Water Quality & Supply
Environment	Mental Health	Women's Ministry
Evangelism & Missions	Microfinance	
Family	Military Support	

This list adapted from "Causes & Passions" by The National Christian Foundation (NCF). www.ncfgiving.com/passions. Published 2022.

The National Christian Foundation has published a useful online experience—"Discover Your Giving Strategy"—at www.ncfgiving.com/solutions/strategy/. Many people find this is a useful tool.

© John Jonez 2024. All Rights Reserved.

ABOUT THE AUTHOR

John Jonez, now retired, spent his career as a financial executive in high-technology companies. With a Master's degree in both Finance and Accounting from the University of Washington, and a Certified Management Accountant Certificate, he is also a published author and was an adjunct instructor of these subjects at the university level.

For over 15 years, John has volunteered as a leader in the areas of Biblical Stewardship and Generosity. With the heart of a teacher, his passion is helping followers of Jesus Christ wrestle with and discover for themselves the relationship between wealth, generosity, and discipleship. He is often requested to teach or facilitate discussions on these topics.

John currently serves as an Executive Board Member for the National Christian Foundation in Austin, Texas. He and his wife Kirsten have served in several different roles at their church, including numerous short-term mission trips to Central America and Africa. They currently live in Leander, Texas.

www.generousheart.com

ACKNOWLEDGMENTS

Starting with the person who influenced me the earliest in my life, and therefore had the most lasting impact, it would undoubtedly be my grandmother. "Gram," as she was known, taught me the value of a dollar, a quarter actually, and the wisdom of saving money, though she had very little. Without a high school diploma, and mired in a life of poverty having tragically lost her husband at an early age, she demonstrated what it meant to live a generous life. Gram would do anything for anyone. When I was five years old, she taught me how to "make change" when her customers came to pick up their orders from her small sewing shop. She was surprised I could do it correctly each time at such a young age, and her customers always double-checked the coins I put in their hand. Gram told me that I'd likely "work with money" in my career, whatever that meant. She was right.

In more recent years, I credit Ryan Assunto, President of the Austin affiliate of the National Christian Foundation, for the wisdom he provided that shaped my own views about generosity in the life of a follower of Jesus.

For the motivation and perseverance to write this book, it has been the weekly Friday mornings spent with my friend Pastor Aaron Foor in his "garage turned office and recording studio," where we brainstormed on his whiteboard, producing many good ideas. He can't think without his whiteboard, and I can't think without my coffee mug in hand, so we worked well together.

In the 15+ years as a volunteer in the area of Biblical Stewardship and Generosity in my church, the team of people I volunteered with, and especially those who took the classes we offered, helped me more than they ever knew. It was their questions or ideas I had never thought of before, and the time spent coaching them through financial difficulties, that dramatically expanded my understanding of the real-world issues.

I am deeply indebted to the leaders and teachers whose work inspired me to delve deeper into these topics, including but certainly not limited to Theo Smith, Pastor of Stewardship, Donna Nicholson Stief, Director of Stewardship at LCBC Church, and Mike Riches, author of *Living Set Free in Christ*.

It was Arlyn Lawrence, of Inspira Literary Solutions, and her team of experts, who added the creative touch to this writing, and her editing transformed my often-clumsy words into clear expressions of my own thoughts. Thank you for your guidance, your spiritual wisdom, and especially your heart in all you do.

It is my deepest hope for everyone who opens this book that it leads to a deeper and more intimate relationship with our Creator.

ENDNOTES

1. Irving, Washington. "The Creole Village," a short story, 1887. Reprinted in The Literature Network. https://www.online-literature.com/irving/crayon-papers/15/
2. Textus Receptus Bibles.
3. Briggs, Dave & Goulard, Chris. *Stewardship Impact Workshop.* Copyright 2023. Presented at the CSN Annual Forum, Fort Lauderdale, FL. March 2023. www.ChristianStewardshipNetwork.com.
4. www.dictionary.com
5. Adams, James Truslow. *The Epic of America.* Little, Brown & Company. New York, NY: 1931. Routledge. New York, NY: 2017. Pp. 415–416.
6. Towner, Dick & Tofilon. *Good Sense Budget Course Participants Guide.* Willow Creek Association. Zondervan. Grand Rapids, IL: 2002.
7. O'Neill, Jessie H. *The Golden Ghetto: The Psychology of Affluence*. The Affluenza Project. Milwaukee, WI: 1997.
8. Chopra, Sanjiv & Vild, Gina. *The Two Most Important Days*. Thomas Dunne Books, St. Martin's Press. New York, NY: 2017. Page 66.
9. White, Alexandria. "73% of Americans Rank Their Finances as the No. 1 Stress in Life." Capital One CreditWise Survey, Published May 20, 2024. Accessed June 9, 2024. https://www.cnbc.com/select/73-percent-of-americans-rank-finances-as-the-number-one-stress-in-life/
10. Ng, Weiting; Diener, E.; Harter, James. *Affluence, Feeling of Stress, and Well-Being.*" Published November 1, 2009. Accessed June 9, 2024.
11. Intuit Credit Karma. "Forget Doom Scrolling; Americans Now Doom Spend to Cope with Stress." Intuit Credit Karma, a study conducted by Qualtrics on behalf of Intuit Credit Karma, published November 2023. Accessed June 9, 2024. https://www.creditkarma.com/about/commentary/forget-doom-scrolling-americans-now-doom-spend-to-cope-with-stress
12. USAFacts.org. "Nearly Half of American Households Have No Retirement Savings." Published Nov 9, 2023. Accessed June 7, 2024. https://usafacts.org/data-projects/retirement-savings
13. Board of Governors of the Federal Reserve System. *Economic Well-Being of U.S. Households in 2023*. Published May 2024. Accessed June 7, 2024. https://www.federalreserve.gov/publications/files/2023-report-economic-well-being-us-households-202405.pdf. Page 32.
14. Craftsman (A Stanley Black and Decker brand). *"Take Back Your Garage: American Garages Store More Clutter than Cars."* Published Nov 1, 2022 by prnewswire.com. Accessed June 7, 2024. https://www.prnewswire.com/news-releases/take-back-your-garage-american-garages-store-more-clutter-than-cars-according-to-craftsman-survey-301664129.html
15. Towner, Dick & Tofilon. *Good Sense Budget Course Participants Guide.* Willow Creek Association. Zondervan. Grand Rapids, IL: 2002.
16. www.dictionary.com
17. www.dictionary.com
18. Anderson, Jeff. *Plastic Donuts*. Waterbrook Multnomah Books, Colorado Springs, CO. Published 2012 & 2013. ISBN 978-1-60142-528-7.
19. United for Alice. https://unitedforalice.org/
20. Quicken.com. *"10 Budget Categories That Belong in Your Plan."* Published February 23, 2024. Accessed June 7, 2024. https://www.quicken.com/blog/budget-categories/
21. *Causes & Passions, How to Identify Where God Is Calling You to Give.* www.ncfgiving.com/passions. Published by The National Christian Charitable Foundation, Inc. 2022.
22. O'Neill, Jessie H. *The Golden Ghetto: The Psychology of Affluence*. The Affluenza Project. Milwaukee, WI: 1997.
23. https://en.wikipedia.org/wiki/Ethan_Couch

www.ingramcontent.com/pod-product-compliance
Lightning Source LLC
Chambersburg PA
CBHW040001080526
44586CB00027B/2842